PRAY FOR RAIN!

The Cure For Drought And Famine Is RAIN!

Dr. Jerry A. Grillo, Jr.

FZM Publishing

Copyright 2008
By Fogzone Ministries
P.O. Box 3707 Hickory, NC. 28603

All Scriptures, unless indicated, are taken from the King James Version

Scriptures quotations marked NJKV are taken from the New King James Version

Scriptures quotations marked NIV are taken from the New International Version.

ISBN
978-0-578-00461-7

Printed in the United States of America.

PRAY FOR RAIN

TABLE OF CONTENT

Special Thanks

First, I want to thank my wonderful family. Maryann, you are the best wife any man could have. Your wisdom and counsel are golden. My two children, Jerry III and Jordan; there are no human words to describe how much I love you. You three make my life worth living every single day.

April Mercer, your dedication and loyalty to helping advance these projects to completion is truly appreciated. I know those who are blessed by these books are very grateful for your dedication and hard work... Your input and changes are an incredible help.

I want to thank my proof readers for taking the time and energy to scrutinize this manuscript to make it a better read.

Darryl Miller-your graphic work and friendship help make every project a joy. Thanks for your skill in making my books look bookstore ready.

To all my partners who sow money and time into my ministry, especially those who are members at The Favor Center, thanks so much for your love and your confidence to allow me to do what I do.

To my parents, you are the greatest... I love spending time with you. Your prayers are very important. Also, to my second set of parents- some call them "in laws," I call them family.

DR. JERRY A. GRILLO, JR.

Foreword

No ministry, no calling, no anointing is without its challenges and adversities.

I often say, ***"The greater the anointing, the greater the trial!"***

In *Pray for Rain,* Dr. Grillo gives the reader an honest glimpse at some of the hidden struggles which we deal with on a daily basis, yet are often reluctant to discuss as candidly as we would like.

The ability to balance the reins of spirituality and humanity is an astounding feat that by all accounts can only be understood by those who've been placed in such a spiritual drought that demands crying out to God, **"Send the rain!"**

By revealing his personal thoughts and struggles and how he continually overcomes them to fulfill the call of God, Dr. Grillo delivers a message of ***endurance, success and accountability*** to the call upon your life that those around you may not readily understand.

After every storm the sun shines and nature continually gives way to growth. And so it is with your spiritual walk. If you can make it through the storm you can look forward to the blessing that accompanies the outpouring of rain.

Many times, the only way to experience your full potential is to be placed in a predicament for your hidden capabilities to be revealed through the clouds. This book is a must read... You are not going to be disappointed in the outcome of your life after the impartation of the information that has been placed between these pages.

Bishop George G. Bloomer
Senior Pastor, Bethel Family Worship Center
Bestselling author, *Witchcraft in the Pews*

Why I Wrote This Book

WHY I WROTE THIS BOOK:

*I*t has been a hard and long journey thus far! In my mind, there seems to be a constant thought that haunts me. That thought is, why Lord? How long Lord? When does trouble stop coming? Have I lost my way? Where is my harvest? What's wrong with me? There are so many more questions. I fear there isn't enough time to write them all. Have you ever felt this way? Have you ever had these same thought patterns?

First, let me make it clear that I understand that you should fight these thoughts and stop them immediately from controlling your emotions. But face it; we all have to fight these kinds of thought patterns. Come on! Let's be real!

REALITY IS FLAWED... ANYTHING UNFLAWED IS AN ILLUSION

Recently, I have been doing some major introspection into my life. I'm 47 years old, at the time of writing this book, and wondering, where has my life gone? Nothing I've planned for has yet come to pass. I have been in ministry now for some twenty plus years.

While I'm writing this I am presently in a mess... I had an eight year staff member leave me with anger and wrong attitudes. *My ministry is in need of a financial break through... My nights have become sleepless torments... To top it off, others are succeeding around me who I know are not doing what they should be doing... Does this sound like I'm complaining?* Well, maybe I am! But it's my book.

This is not complaining. This is me being real. Like you've never had the same thoughts and if we try to talk to others we seem to always get the Christian Clichés. I've decided to stop hiding what so many try to act like they don't think or feel. Especially not while I'm writing this book; you the reader matter to me and this is my attempt to set things right in your life as well as mine.

While we are on this introduction let me give you some advice. Crying out to your spouse or those around you about your pain will never fix it at all.

I was sitting in the bed one night with silent frustration, flipping from channel to channel, when I caught this woman speaking on TBN. She said something that ministered to me. She said she was in need of something that would help her worship at a different level. While she was speaking, I could sense the Spirit of the Lord increasing in my room.

She elaborated on how she had found a CD of David and Nicole Binion. The song she heard that dropped her to the floor was the song, **"Pray for Rain."** When she began to sing a part of the song..... *"When you don't know what to do... Pray for rain."* *"When your life is full of doubt... Pray for rain..."*

I began to sense a feeling of peace come over me. I got up the next day singing all day, *"Lord, send the rain!"* I can't begin to tell you how that prayer and statement began to calm the storm within me. Here's the strangest thing, to pray for rain means that there has to be storm clouds overhead. When you're in a crisis, and all you see is storm clouds all about you; lift up your face and get ready, it's about to rain!

So, I did what I do. I went to the office and looked up every scripture on the word 'rain.' The word 'rain' appears one hundred-two times in the King James Bible. I have gone through all the verses and have compiled the information in this book to help you prepare for your next season.

There's about to be a season of an incredible

outpouring! God is about to open the windows of Heaven and pour out His rain; not just a sprinkle or a mist. He's about to give you an outpouring….an abundance of rain!

Get ready! Prepare yourself. I believe that this book is going to bring to your life the rains of healing, prosperity and joy. Whether you need a marital touch, a financial touch or an emotional touch, when it rains, you're going to experience the refreshing touch of the Spirit of God in all areas of your life.

Listen, do you hear it? I hear the sound of the abundance of rain.

Let me ask you a few questions before we dive into this book.

- Are you willing to do whatever it takes to change?
- Are you willing to do whatever it takes to be set free?
- What are you willing to walk away from to allow God to walk back into your life?
- Are you fed up with the mundane?
- Would you like more; more money, a better life, greater relationships…?

If so, then get ready for it! Grab a Bible and a notebook and take this book and read it as a daily devotional. Use it as a manual for change. I promise that when you're finished you're going to get soaking wet with God's presence.

Don't be afraid to change. Don't be afraid to allow the Spirit to move on and over you. Ask the Holy Spirit right now to help you. He is alive and wants to be your counselor, mentor and friend.
While I was at Bishop Jeff Poole's opening of his new church facilities in Warner Robins, Georgia, God spoke a word to my heart through the Man of God who is the spiritual father of Bishop Jeff Poole. The message that Pastor Clint Brown spoke that night resonated through my spirit man like an arrow moving through the air. **No More Portions**! This was his message.

That it's possible to be freed from the hand of bondage but still be in bondage to the land. So when God was ready to deliver His people He had to take them out of the land of Egypt to a land that was already occupied with the enemy. This was God's way of forcing them to fight for what they wanted.

The same is true for the spiritual rain of heaven. If you want it you are going to have to do something to get it.

Take the time necessary to extract the information placed within these pages. My prayer for your life is that by the end of this book, no by the end of this day, God will begin to open the windows of heaven and pour His rain upon you.

I'm asking God to let it rain... Rain over your finances... Rain over your children... Rain over your marriage...Rain over your mind, your health and your desires.

Thank you for reading this book!

Jerry Grillo

CHAPTER ONE

PREPARE FOR THE OUTPOURING!

DR. JERRY A. GRILLO, JR.

Posture Yourself for the Abundance of Rain...

"And every plant of the field before it was in the earth, and every herb of the field before it grew: for the LORD God had not caused it to rain upon the earth, and there was not a man to till the ground. 6 but there went up a mist from the earth, and watered the whole face of the ground."
Genesis 2:5-6

The first thing we must understand about creation is that for anything to grow on the earth, it needs water. Water is the life source of all living things. Water determines how large, or how small, things will be.

After God made the earth and all living creatures, He had to establish a way to supply the earth with moisture, water. To supply the earth with the life source of water, God creates a system whereby the dew, or *mist*, would fall each day. The *mist* would supply the earth with what it needed to maintain what had already been planted by God. At this point, there had been no plowing, no sowing of seeds and no reaping of a harvest. Just enough water to maintain what God had established. There's no telling how long the earth had been here. No life on earth can exist without water, and the ceaseless flow of that water cannot exist without rain. The earth was being watered by way of a *mist*... God would not open the heavens and pour out rain because He lacked one major ingredient. He had no man, no person in place that could till the soil when the heavens opened. Unless there is a seed planted for the rain to produce a harvest and a man to till and work the soil for the harvest, God will not let it rain.

Let me ask you a serious question. If God could do what He was doing with a *mist*, or dew, what could He do with an outpouring? If God has been using a *mist* to do what He's done in your life, what could you be experiencing living in and walking in, if the heavens opened their resources and it rained?

Think for a moment about what the *mist* represents. It's enough of God's resource to maintain and keep the minimum supplied, to produce minimum results and have minimum power. Sounds just like the twenty-first century church to me. What do you think? The *mist* represents the mediocrity of not wanting to do more... know more... experience more. It's the mindset that you should be thankful for what you have and never expect more. Well, I'm sorry, but I'm not satisfied. Yes, I am thankful for what I have, but the truth is, I want more! I don't want to experience a *mist*, I want an outpouring! I want more! There, I said it! I want more of God's presence. I want more money. I want my life to count for more... I want my children to have more, my wife, my entire family to experience more! I want my church to have more!

I want better! I want the people around me to increase and have more. I want them to learn more... know more... pray more... worship more. I am sick and tired of this limp wrist, weak willed attitude that has crept into the people of God. Let's start desiring an outpouring! I've had enough of the *mist*! How about you? Are you going to desire more? Do you want more? Well, if you do, then wouldn't you want to know how to open the windows of heaven so you can experience the outpouring of God's love and abundance?

Get ready. I know without a shadow of a doubt that we are living close to the entry of Jesus and the exodus of His church. There has to be one last wave of His glory before the end comes. God is about to open the heavens and pour out His Spirit in flood proportions. So much so, that there will not be room enough for you to contain it.

THE MIST IS OVER, THE OUTPOURING IS HERE!

Stop looking for this outpouring to come, it's already here! We are not waiting on God, God is waiting on us. He's waiting for man to get in position for this outpouring. Let's look at a verse that gives clarity to this first chapter. Right off the bat, I want to build an expectation for you to start believing for rain. WE NEED RAIN!

"The end of a thing is better than its beginning..."
Ecclesiastes 7:8 NKJV

If the end of a thing is better than its beginning then think for a moment about how the church began. Think of all the power Jesus walked in. The church and Jesus are the starting point. In the early church, there was no lack found among them. They saw great

WHEN YOU ARE IN THE RIGHT ENVIRONMENT YOUR GENIUS WILL MATERIALIZE

miracles... blind eyes seeing... deaf ears hearing... lame legs walking and so on. Now, I also know they suffered great persecution, but this is not my focus at this point. Look at all the power, the commitment level, the love and abundance the church walked in. That's how it began. If it began with such power, how much greater is it going to end, seeing that the end of a thing is better than its beginning? Can you already sense the climate around you changing? **Do you feel the moisture in the air...? Yes you do, it's about to rain!** Even while I'm writing, I am fighting back tears of praise. I am about to explode with shouts of joy! The outpouring is here! We just need to unlock it.

POSITION MATTERS FOR AN OUTPOURING TO HAPPEN:

Posture is very important. Posture is a part of manners. We are taught by our parents and then by our mentors, for success. My father was a stickler for posture and manners. If you slouched over while you were walking, he would shout, "Stand up!" If you scuffed your feet, he would shout, "Pick up your feet!" If you brought your mouth to your plate, he would say, "Bring your spoon, or fork to your mouth, not your mouth to your food." Everyday my mother would check our teeth, inspect our hands, and smell our hair, to make sure that we had washed. Now, all this was absolute nonsense to me as a child, but when I became a man and had my own children, I realized that my parents taught us manners, not because they didn't love us, or wouldn't accept us, but manners and posture were taught to us so if we were in someone else's atmosphere we would be accepted. I, in turn, have taught manners to my children. Manners will give you access to the atmosphere of others. Blessings from others are released to those who have great manners. *Such as; "Yes Ma'am"..."No Sir"... "May I Please?"* The same is true with God. When He sees us in the position He has assigned for us, He will open the windows of heaven and we will be blessed.

YOU MUST BE WHERE YOU ARE ASSIGNED TO BE:
First, we must understand that just having the right manners, the right words and the right confessions, is not enough. You have to be in the right posture and in the right place. Maybe our prayer needs to be less about what God can give us and more about where God wants to place us. Seek the Holy Spirit to teach you the right position. **Reposition** yourself to be ready to receive this move of His glory. Place yourself in a position that will cause the windows of heaven to open. When that window is open why don't you shout, "Let it rain! I'm ready for it."

PLACES MATTER
There were places before there were people. Geography matters to God. You must be in the right place. You can be the right person in the wrong place and heaven will stay closed. Now remember, you may be experiencing the mist and the mist is pretty good, but it's not the best. You must be the right person, in the right place, at the right time. Until you find

that place, you will only experience the mist of God.

When does God open the window of heaven for Jesus?

> *"And it came to pass in those days that Jesus came from Nazareth of Galilee, and was baptized of John in Jordan. And straightway coming up out of the water, he saw the heavens opened, and the Spirit like a dove descending upon him: And there came a voice from heaven, saying, Thou art my beloved Son, in whom I am well pleased."*
> *Mark 1:9-11*

In Isaiah 9:6, it says that unto us a child is given, unto us a son is born... Now when did Jesus stop being a child and start being a Son? When He was in position, and when He was where He was supposed to be. When God saw Jesus coming up from the water, at the age of 30, He called Jesus Son! Then, Jesus experienced the open heavens of God's love and blessing. He walked in an outpouring because He was where He was supposed to be. The same is true for us. When God looks over heaven and He sees us in position. When He sees us in His place, where He has been leading us all of our lives, that's when the heavens open and God speaks to us about our destiny. Look at what God said, "This is my Son, in whom I am well pleased." Now wait a minute. Up until that point, Jesus really hadn't done anything. Yet, God was pleased. Could it be, that when we are where we are suppose to be, even if to us, it's a place of drought, storms, and crisis, that God is pleased? Why is He so pleased? Because He knows that life in the mist is over and the outpouring life has now begun. Listen, do you hear it? Do you hear the sound of the abundance of rain?

PLACES BEFORE PEOPLE: GEOGRAPHY MATTERS!

> *"Then the word of the LORD came to him, saying, "Get away from here and turn eastward, and hide by the*

*Brook Cherith, which flows into the Jordan. And it will be that you shall drink from the brook, and I have commanded the ravens to feed you **there**." 1 Kings 17:2-5 NKJV*

The prophet Elijah could have gone anywhere he wanted, but the blessing of provision was scheduled for one place. If you never discover where *there* is, you will never discover the true prosperity of God. Blessings aren't following you... Money doesn't follow you. Blessings are waiting on you. They are where you are assigned to be. The raven would come everyday to feed the man of God. If he wasn't where he was supposed to be, guess what? You guessed it! He would have starved. He would have gone thirsty. How many of God's children are starving and thirsty simply because they refuse to discover where *there* is?

> **The Instruction You Are Willing To Follow, Creates the Future You Are Able To Walk In**
> *Mike Murdock*

Pray all you want! Confess every verse in the Bible... Go to conference after conference. Jump from church to church. No matter what you do, you will only experience the mist. You were not made to live on the mist. You were created for an outpouring, but you have to be in the right place.

Notice what kind of bird God used to feed the man of God, a raven. In that culture, the raven was a dirty bird... it represented a curse. The raven was considered to be a cursed bird. What kind of animal did God choose to use? Not an eagle, not even a dove. No, He used a raven. When you are in your assigned place, God will have the curse that was supposed to kill you, the enemy that was supposed to destroy you, be the very thing that sustains you in times of drought and hardship. At the end of an instruction, God has scheduled your miracle. The difference between dying in the wilderness of hunger and feasting everyday by the brook is a simple instruction. The instructions you are willing to follow, creates the future you are able to walk in.

GODLY INSTRUCTIONS ARE SEASONAL:

> *"And it came to pass **after a while,** that the brook dried up, because there had been no rain in the land. And the word of the LORD came unto him, saying, Arise, get thee to Zarephath, which belongeth to Zidon, and dwell there: behold, I have commanded a widow woman there to sustain thee." 1 Kings 17:7-9*

After a while, a season, the brook dried up and the raven quit coming. We must understand that seasons can, and must, change. One of the reasons so many Christians are dried up, hungry and thirsty is because they won't let God do something different in their church. The minute the pastor decides to do something different, or change things up, the body gets mad and wants to stop the process of change. Heaven forbid, if we expect God to do something different, or change.

The outpouring of blessing is tied to the ability to recognize the Words of God for change. Instructions are not always permanent, they can be, but they can also change.

SEQUENCE MATTERS:

> *"**So he arose and went** to Zarephath. And when he came to the gate of the city, behold, the widow woman was there gathering of sticks: and he called to her, and said, Fetch me, I pray thee, a little water in a vessel, that I may drink. And as she was going to fetch it, he called to her, and said, Bring me, I pray thee, a morsel of bread in thine hand."*
> *1 Kings 17:10-11*

A crisis doesn't make a person, it reveals them. Here was a major famine, and to have a famine, there had to be a shortage of rain. The Lord had held up the rain, and the land had become useless, dead and barren. It doesn't matter how much seed is in the soil. If it doesn't rain, the seed and the soil are useless. Remember that! Sowing is not enough; there must be rain from heaven.

Doesn't it strike you odd that God told Elijah that He had commanded the widow to feed him, yet, Elijah is the one telling her to fetch him some water and to make him a cake... FIRST? What really confuses me is the speed at which the widow responds to fetching the water. Yet, when she is asked to bring him a morsel of bread, she hesitates. What has been withheld from heaven? Rain! That makes water the most precious seed she has, yet, she's having a meltdown over the bread. So she tries to explain to the prophet that there is just enough for her and her son.

> *"And she said, As the LORD thy God liveth, I have not a cake, but an handful of meal in a barrel, and a little oil in a cruse: and, behold, I am gathering two sticks, that I may go in and dress it for me and my son, that we may eat it, and die." 1 Kings 17:12*

She had enough faith for today. She had none for tomorrow. When God asks you for a seed, it's not today He has on his mind, but tomorrow. Oh God, let it rain! Open the windows of heaven and rain on my seed! Rain on my marriage! We desire an outpouring. We are tired of the mist!

TO SURVIVE YOUR DROUGHT YOU MUST BE WILLING TO HEAR GOD'S VOICE COMING THROUGH A MAN OF GOD.

"For thus saith the LORD God of Israel, The barrel of meal shall not waste, neither shall the cruse of oil fail, until the day that the LORD sendeth rain upon the earth." 1 Kings 17:13-16

You will miss a lot of God's voice and instruction if you are just sitting around waiting for God to speak to you alone. Trust me; it is not Biblical to think that God alone is going to speak to you and not those He has placed over you. When you sense God is speaking to you, go and seek mentorship from the man of God you sit under. Don't seek mentorship from a friend. That is the blind leading the blind.

TO SURVIVE YOUR DROUGHT IT WILL REQUIRE SOMETHING FROM YOUR HAND TO BE RELEASED. *"And Elijah said unto her, Fear not; go and do as thou hast said:* **but make me thereof a little cake first**, *and bring it unto me and after make for thee and for thy son." 1 Kings 17:13-16*

WHEN YOU SOW YOUR SEED (CAKE), REMEMBER THERE IS A SUPERNATURAL HARVEST ATTACHED TO IT. *"And she went and did according to the saying of Elijah: and she, and he, and her house, did eat many days. And the barrel of meal wasted not, neither did the cruse of oil fail, according to the word of the LORD, which he spake by Elijah." 1 Kings 17:13-16*

Her meal barrel never ran out, nor did her cruse of oil ever run dry during the entire famine. That's not all; her water supply never ceased either. What a miracle harvest of God's outpouring!

"Pray for rain when your life is void and empty... Pray for rain when your heart is dry and thirsty... pray for rain when you don't know what to say... pray for rain..." David and Nicole Binion

If you want to experience what this widow experienced then you must be willing to do what she did.

First, she recognized that the man speaking to her wasn't just a man. He was Man of God! She must have understood that He was a golden key. This man possessed something greater.

Second, she had to be willing to see beyond her famine and loss. She had the ability to look to the harvest instead of the seed she was about to release. The sense of loss will always try to enter; fight this feeling because you will reap as she did if you faint not.

Third, she was willing to follow the instruction. She obeyed and trusted in the words of the Man of God.

Even Abraham needed the Man of God to bring him to a different level of promise. Abraham had the promise but through his connection and recognition of Melchizedek the high priest, his life changed from just having the promise and blessing, to being under a protection and being blessed.

When Abraham tithed to Melchizedek, he tithed up. This recognition and releasing of his money brought him to an even greater dimension of promise. The rain of protection and covering was released.

The Man of God over you is your golden connection to your next dimension. Don't let anyone talk you away from the church and Man of God you have connected to. Only God can sever that connection, and when He does, He always does it in order.

HOW TO LEAVE ONE PLACE FOR THE RIGHT PLACE:

I have been a pastor for years, and one of the greatest problems in the church is how people just up and leave after they've made commitments to join membership. Most of them leave out of order. When we leave the wrong way we create in our lives a season of no protection.

For instance, I had this family come to The Favor Center. When they came their marriage and family were in a mess. Mind you these people had been in church for 20 years. They came to me with marital mess. The wife had somewhat cheated on her husband... the kids were in disorder... I spent hours talking to them... and in a few years their family seemed to be coming together. After we did the work to bring restoration to this family, they just hopped up and left.

Here's where they have messed up in my opinion. They sent me an email, a paragraph letting me know that the Lord was directing them away from The Favor Center. So I responded to them with an email and asked why I didn't even deserve a phone call or visit. They began to inform me that the Lord directed them to do it that way. Come on! How stupid.

When you leave a place... Please leave properly. Because how you leave a season determines how you enter the next season...

Go and talk to the man of God and explain to him why... Don't spiritualize your decision if it's not a spiritual reason. Maybe you just don't like the way that church sets up their services or preaching. You know what? **That's ok**! But to say God told you to leave, without an explanation is wrong. I believe it causes you to enter your next season unprotected and unproductive.

If you have left a ministry wrong this could be the reason the rain of heaven has stop pouring over your life. Fix it fast. You need the rain of heaven to fall in your life

Document Your Journey

TOPIC	THOUGHT

CHAPTER TWO

SPIRITUAL DEHYDRATION
Are you Hungry or Thirsty?

Spiritual Dehydration
Are you Hungry or Thirsty?

*C*ould you be in need of a drink? Maybe what you really need is not another sermon or preaching tape to listen to; maybe what you need is for God to rain the water of His Spirit over your life. When you lack water, you lack the very substance that makes all the other gifts work. Water, in the Bible, always represents the Spirit of God. Water is the life source of everything on the earth. Water is what the Holy Spirit is in our life. He is the life source to all that God has for us. Without Him, we are dry and thirsty.

The Holy Spirit is the most misunderstood part of the gospel. Is He only in us if we speak in tongues? The answer is no. If no, then we have to deal with the question, has speaking in tongues left the church? The answer to this is again, no. But can we function without speaking in tongues? Yes. Do we need the power of tongues today? Once again, yes! Let me encourage you to seek all of the gifts, not just one. While you're seeking the gift, seek the Giver of the gift and not the gift itself. Go ahead, take a drink. Try for once to allow the Holy Spirit to reveal the water, and when He does, don't close up the window of your faith. Let the rain of heaven fall! The Bible speaks of rain over one hundred-two times. Rain is necessary!

Are You Hungry or are you Thirsty?

I was reading a magazine the other day and an article caught my attention. The article was about dehydration. It stated that most Americans are not getting enough water. One reason for this is because there are so many substitutes such as soda, tea, juice, coffee, etc. These drinks create a false sense of hydration.

Because many people lack water in their body, some that feel they are hungry, may actually be thirsty. This article stated that many are overweight because they are satisfying their hunger pains with food, when actually; they are not hungry at all, but thirsty. The next time you have hunger pains, drink a glass of water. If the hunger pains leave, then you weren't hungry at all, but thirsty. Feeding yourself food is not the answer. Water is the answer.

While I was reading, the Holy Spirit began to deal with me. I heard the question in my head. Could the church be thirsty? Could it be that we are satisfied with food, when what we really need is for God to open the window of Heaven and give us a spiritual drink?

Symptoms of dehydration:
Thirst, dry mouth, sunken eyes, weak pulse, skin loses its elasticity and isn't supple, cold hands and feet, confusion, lethargy, difficulty in being aroused... This sounds like the condition of some churches to me. We don't need another sermon. We need an outpouring! We need God to send the rain of His Spirit!

Didn't Paul warn us about the last days? Didn't Paul mentor Timothy that there would be these kinds of thirsty believers, who would have the form, but deny the water? They would look like those who had a holy life. They would even appear to be righteous, but in the end would deny the power, the water and the Spirit. I think he did.

"...always learning but never able to acknowledge the truth. Just as Jannes and Jambres opposed Moses, so also these men oppose the truth-men of depraved minds, who, as far as the faith is concerned, are rejected. but

they will not get very far because, as in the case of those men, their folly will be clear to everyone." 2 Timothy 3:7-9 NIV

The proof you are spiritually hydrated is that you have the power to endure. ***Endurance is the proof that you have not just been eating, but you've also been drinking.*** *Water is the key source for power. Let me explain it this way. Too much Word and no Spirit will cause you to dry up. Too much Spirit and no Word will cause you to blow up, but if you have a balance of Word and Spirit, you will grow up!*

- *Endurance is a qualifier.*
- *Endurance decides longevity.*
- *Endurance defeats false witnesses.*
- *Endurance forces the hidden agenda to be revealed.*
- *Those who've endured have the right to be heard.*

Endurance means to be lasting, permanent and durable.

Drinking is not enough. Eating is not enough. For the physical body to be healthy, it needs a balance of the right foods and the proper amount of water. You also have to exercise the body if you want it to stay strong and mobile. Of course, there are more intense things we must do, but this is not a book about health; well, not physical health. This is a book about

Those Who Have Endured Have the Right to Be Heard

ending your spiritual drought. It is a book that is designed to open the windows of Heaven so that you can experience the abundance of God's rain (reign).

Let's put first things first. You can live longer without food than you can without water. Water is more vital than food. Spirit, is first and foremost, vital for the food (Word) to find a place where it will cause you to change and grow. More than once, the

Word of God uses an important phrase about hearing. *"He that hath an ear, let him hear what the Spirit saith unto the churches..." Revelation 2:7*

Someone once said that man can live thirty days without food but only seven days without water. You can't live for more than seven days without water. Water is three times more important than food, yet food is what we spend most of our time stuffing into our mouths. The same is true in the spiritual realm. Why do we eat more and drink less? Maybe because food satisfies more; it satisfies our taste buds. Our emotions are affected by certain foods. Food is a stimulus; whereas, water really has no taste. Water is just for substance. Water is the life source of the body. Water is neutral! It doesn't affect the emotions, it affects the body. I believe the same is true in the supernatural. The preaching of the Word is good, but it also feeds the emotions. The Word, in itself, can be tasty. Someone who is animated can preach and have you crying, laughing and shouting all in one message. It is through preaching that the ears of people are stimulated. If we are not careful, the water of the Word will be ignored. Water has no taste. It has no *pizzazz*, it only has the power to fill and nourish. It's very easy to believe that we are hungry, when in fact, we are actually thirsty.

Too Much Word and You'll dry up! Too Much spirit and you'll blow up... The right mixture of Word and Spirit you'll grow up!

This reminds me of a story about a woman who was living in a time when being of mixed race was really looked down upon. This story takes place in John chapter four, where a certain woman, had been living in the worst of the worst of times. First of all, she was half Jew and half Philistine. This woman lived over two thousand years ago in a city called Sychar, in a place called Samaria.

I believe that everyday, this woman was crying out to God. Knowing that she was forbidden to go to the local church, she had to cry out in her pain. Maybe she was asking God if half of her would be enough to fix her. She knew that one half of her blood line had always been at war with God. What about the other half? Could that part of her be enough; the part of her that was from the race of God? Would God give that part rain? The answer is absolutely! While Jesus was on a journey; He made an effort to go by the way of Samaria. While He was waiting at Jacobs well, this woman came to Him. He had been sitting there watching her climb the mountainside to get to the well that she had drank from most of her life. Today would be different. Today would be the day someone would dip in their well to give her a drink of real, supernatural water. The rain was about to fall in her life.

> *"Jesus answered and said unto her, If thou knewest the gift of God, and who it is that saith to thee, Give me to drink; thou wouldest have asked of him, and he would have given thee living water..." John 4:10*

This woman was dehydrated:

Think for a moment. The Bible says she was married five times and the sixth man she was just living with. If you understand her culture, you would know that women couldn't divorce their husbands. However, if a man was tired of you, he could take you out in the street and declare that you were no longer married to him.

This woman had experienced the deepest power of rejection. First, she was raised a Samaritan which caused her to experience rejection by her peers. Second, she could have been raised in a home with no father image to accept her and give her what she needed to build a healthy and secure identity. Third, she had tried to fill the void of rejection with the presence of men, but these men used her until they were tired of her and then they would throw her out.

She had settled into a pattern of just living with whomever and whatever would accept her at the time, but this day her life was about to change. She was about to experience the rain. God was about to end her drought.

She had to accept that her life could be different; that in the water, the Spirit, there is enough of God to stop the drought. This water is supplied by the rain of heaven. This water would cause her to never thirst again. **<u>This was living water</u>**. She was living in a place where sin abounds... but through her willingness to drink from what Jesus was offering her, she was about to experience that *grace abounds much more*. She was about to change. Without this kind of rain, there will never be any real change. Without this kind of spirit present, at best all we will have is good church. But she needed more than just truth. She needed more than just a good sermon; she needed to drink of the water and the spirit that was present to fix her completely, inside and out.

Do you want to know how she was fixed? Too many are sitting in their pain, in their dry place, waiting on God to make it better. The truth is that if you want to get fixed, you have to **<u>be willing to fix it</u>**! Jesus alone was not going to heal her; she had to be willing to get involved if she was going to receive the Living Water.

She had to be willing to dip in her well and fetch Him some water. I believe that this is not just referring to the well in which there is water, but the well that is full of her life's pain.

If you don't want to dip in the well of your pain and wounds one more time, God is not going to open His never ending supply of water to you. When you dip in this well, you cannot do what you have been doing for so long, which is, drink from it. No, you have to be willing to give this drink to Jesus. When you can give it to Him, He will make the exchange and give you what is in His well. **When she let go, God let go, and rain fell from heaven; rain that never ran out.**

For us to experience this kind of rain. We are going to have to give God what is in our well the same way this woman did. The well represents those things in our lives we are leaving in our past. Give up what's been hurting us... who has rejected us... who let us down, or left us to die. When we let go, we begin to change the atmosphere.

EIGHT AREAS THAT CAN STOP THE RAIN:
1. *Your racial issues*
2. *Wrong relationship*
3. *Unforgiveness*
4. *Bitterness*
5. *Unwillingness to face your past*
6. *Religiosity*
7. *Your condition (wounds)*
8. *Your inability to recognize Jesus*

Document Your Journey

TOPIC	THOUGHT

CHAPTER THREE

EVERY STORM IS PREGNANT WITH CHANGE

"The cloud that sits over your head could be full of blessings and not destruction"

EVERY STORM IS PREGNANT WITH CHANGE

*a*s I mentioned earlier, the Bible speaks about rain one hundred-two times. The first time rain was mentioned, it was about why there had been no rain on the earth. The first time it actually rained, now that's a different picture. The first rain wasn't the rain of blessing or a harvest rain. It wasn't a rain that would end a long drought. It was a rain of judgment.

> *"For yet seven days, and I will cause it to rain upon the earth forty days and forty nights; and every living substance that I have made will I destroy from off the face of the earth." Genesis 7:4*

God had become so angry with the sin of mankind that He decided to start over with just one family and a few animals that were on the ark that Noah built. I was pondering this first rain. Talk about a storm! We have seen news reports of storms, tidal waves, and hurricanes that have devastated places on the earth. In 2005, hurricane Katrina hit the gulf coast and caused much pain and confusion. The people in New Orleans were devastated and felt rejected and abandoned. I remember watching the news and thinking that what I was seeing looked like a third world country, not a city in America. Yet, no

Every Storm Cloud... Could Be Pregnant With Promise

~33~

matter how horrific it was, and I know it was, it doesn't even touch the storm in Genesis chapter eight. This rain, this storm, wasn't just in one place; this storm covered the whole earth! Not one mountain was left uncovered. Every living thing was destroyed. God covered the earth in forty days. The rain that fell from the sky that day wasn't like the rain we see today. It didn't rain in little drops, it rained in sheets. Lake size, ocean size drops fell from heaven.

At the end of this horrible judgment, after the sun came out and Noah was sitting on the wet soil, God said, "I will never again destroy the earth with water". He also placed a rainbow over the clouds as a sign of His promise. The first covenant God made with man was a covenant birthed from judgment.

MOST RAIN IS HIDDIN IN STORM CLOUDS:

When I was praying for spiritual rain I began to ask God to let it rain and the Holy Spirit so gently asked me, *"Do you really want it to rain, son?"* I replied, *"Yes, I do!"* *"Then you must first expect it to become cloudy for it to rain, I must first send you a storm."* Every cloud is pregnant with rain. For us to experience the promise and rain of blessing, we are going to have to live through some storms. Crisis and circumstances don't make us, they reveal us.

Storms Are A Part of Life! Get use to it.

Storms are a part of life. Crises are going to happen. Someone once said, *"You are either in a crisis, coming out of a crisis, or getting ready to enter a crisis."* Crisis, pain, problems and storms are always going to show up in our lives.

"And the LORD smelled a sweet savour; and the LORD said in his heart, I will not again curse the ground any more for man's sake; for the imagination of man's heart is evil from his youth; neither will I again smite any more every thing living, as I have done." Genesis 8:21

Expect crisis. Prepare for them. The Hebrew word for crisis is translated **"birthing stool."** The Hebrew children understood that crisis is the curve of change. When they faced trouble, they called their trouble Meshba, a place where God could birth new things! Every storm cloud is pregnant with your blessing. Storm clouds are nothing more than your blessing in disguise.

Can you sense your miracle in the atmosphere? Listen, I hear the sound of the abundance of rain! Your rain is about to fall! Get ready for the downpour of healing, blessing, increase, prosperity and joy!

When the sun stops shining and is no longer visible, remember that it is still shining on the other side of the clouds that have blocked it for a season. But, while the sun is blocked, guess what, the rain is about to fall. So lift up your hands in the midst of your storm, lift your face to the sky and get ready to feel the refreshing sprinkle of your harvest, your promotion and your blessing. Get ready for the rain! Let it pour!

FACTS ABOUT PROBLEMS:

1. Problems are the gates to your significance.
2. Problems are seeds for change.
3. Problems link you to your golden connections.
4. Problems provide you with income.... Income and money are attached to a problem.
5. Problems birth opportunities. God never told David to fight Goliath... Others saw a problem, David saw opportunity.
6. Problems can identify your uniqueness.
7. Problems will reveal your enemies.
8. Problems identify your friends.

Remove crisis, remove problems, and lose the power of connection. Our mess connects us to someone who can help us. After you have survived your mess, you will turn it into your message. Look at the spelling of the word 'message'...

"**Message**" Add age... time to a mess, you have the word message... The proof you have a message is how you survived your crisis.

Let me encourage you, there will be times when you will feel no advancement. We all have had those days where if feels like no matter what you are not making head way. In times of crisis, you are not always going to move forward. In those times you will have to survive.

MOTION IS RELEVANT TO PERCEPTION:

The law of motion is that "motion is relevant to perception." For example, if you were riding in a car going sixty miles per hour, and at the same time, you were holding a book in your hand, the book would appear, in your eyes, as if it was standing still; however; you understand by looking out the window, that you are moving at sixty miles per hour. Now, if I were standing on the roadside watching you pass by, both you and the book would be moving at sixty miles per hour. In my perception, both are moving, but in your perception, the only one moving is you. Motion is relevant to perception.

It appears by perception that sometimes you are moving and that you have stagnated in your life. This doesn't mean you're not moving. Your perception has become distorted. The key to motion is perception. In God's world perception is always reality. When you appear to not be moving in the natural in God's perception you are moving. God sees you moving toward your destiny. This is the reason you must survive your pain. Even though you think you're not moving, you really are!

God used the storm of in Noah's life to create a promise for us to understand the law of the earth. The clouds that were schedule for judgment were also pregnant with promise for those who survived them.

"...The rainbow shall be in the cloud, and I will look on it to remember the everlasting covenant between God and

every living creature of all flesh that is on the earth."
Genesis 9:16-17 NKJV

The first covenant given to man was directly related to the first storm ever recorded. God said that He would place a rainbow in the clouds as a sign that no matter how bad and wicked the clouds looked, He wasn't going to destroy the earth again with rain. I use to live in Central Florida, and in the summer, around evening time, there would come the most terrible looking clouds and thunderstorms that would cause the hair on your arms to stand up. I remember looking up one day and seeing the most beautiful rainbow between two of the darkest clouds. Right in the midst of the storm was God's covenant.

How does God create a rainbow? He uses the mist of the rain in the storm. How is God going to give you a rainbow? He's going to use the mist of rain within your storm. One more thing, it was right after the storm that God gave us a glimpse into one of His secrets.

"While the earth remaineth, **seedtime and harvest,** *and cold and heat, and summer and winter, and day and night* **shall not cease***" Genesis 8:21-22*

*"**And God blessed** Noah and his sons, and said unto them, be fruitful, and multiply, and replenish the earth." Genesis 9:1*

The first thing that Noah did to be blessed was sow a seed and plant a vineyard. Think about this for a moment. God's goal was to destroy every living thing during the flood. The only living thing that survived was what was placed in the Ark. God destroyed everything with water, but here's the catch. Everything was destroyed, but the seed that was placed in the soil. The seed was never touched. After the storm when the water receded and the sun hit the soil, immediately the seed woke up and began to replenish the earth.

Here's a thought. Could the clouds and storms in your life be the very agent that will cause dormant seeds in your life to come to fruition?

> Joseph said to them, "Do not be afraid, for am I in the place of God? But as for you, you meant evil against me; but God meant it for good, in order to bring it about as it is this day, to save many people alive." Genesis 50:19-21 NKJV

I wanted to end this chapter with this verse. If anyone had the right to be bitter over the storms of life it was Joseph. God gave him a dream of his future. God showed Joseph that he would one day be and do great things, but Joseph experienced great crisis on his journey.

God reveals your future but never your journey: If God would have told Joseph what he would have to travel through to fulfill His dreams, Joseph may have never wanted to enter his future. God will always give us a word in the beginning of our journey, but never reveal the storms we are going to have to survive to fulfill them.

I believe the reason God does this is so when the storm clouds become dark and scary, and the wind begins to blow, you will find refuge in the promise He gave you in the beginning.

The storm may not be blowing you off course, but on course to your destiny. Everything that happened in Joseph's life was preparing him to sit second to the greatest king of his time. He had to survive the clouds, the rain and the storms of life to be able to sit in a seat that would have as much power as the king. No one was higher than Joseph in the end, no one except the king.

Joseph maintained the heart of his dream in the midst

of his greatest storms. The verse I used reveals the heart that Joseph kept through the whole ordeal of being betrayed by his brothers, sold into slavery, lied about by his master's wife and thrown into prison for four years. Here's the power of storm clouds. What they were meant to do, destroy and create havoc in your life, God will turn it toward your good. He uses problems to create doors and passageways to your future. Every cloud could be pregnant with your promotion.

How did Joseph survive those years of pain? He never allowed what was happening to him affect what God was doing in him.

Joseph never discussed his pain to any one, only his dreams. There is no where in the story where we can find Joseph complaining to anyone about his crisis. He never discussed what his brothers did to him while he was in Potiphar's house. He never discussed the false accusation he went through while he was in prison. As a matter of fact, you never read that he talked about how he didn't belong in prison. What blows my mind is how quickly Joseph is promoted in prison.

> *"But the Lord was with Joseph and showed him mercy, and He gave him favor in the sight of the keeper of the prison. And the keeper of the prison committed to Joseph's hand all the prisoners who were in the prison; whatever they did there, it was his doing. The keeper of the prison did not look into anything that was under Joseph's authority, because the Lord was with him; and whatever he did, the Lord made it prosper."* Genesis 39:21-40:1 NKJV

Joseph was promoted because he kept his heart from anger and complaint. He believed in the rain that was housed in the storm clouds that had been hovering over his life. I believe the same is true for you and me. We just have to do what Joseph did. When we keep our dreams alive in the midst of the most terrible howling winds and crisis, God can promote us in the end. No matter how dark his life appeared, not one time did Joseph appear to lose his faith in his future and have a pity party. He maintained a mind and attitude of excellence. Thus he was promoted to keeper of the prison.

The countenance of others mattered to Joseph. There were two men thrown into prison. They were the butler and baker who served the king. One day Joseph noticed that there faces looked sad.

> *"And Joseph came in to them in the morning and looked at them, and saw that they were sad. So he asked Pharaoh's officers who were with him in the custody of his lord's house, saying,* **"Why do you look so sad today?"** *Genesis 40:6-7 NKJV*

This shows me that no matter what was happening in the life of Joseph he wasn't buying into it with his heart and mind. He was a caring person in the middle of the hardest places. Others mattered to him. You will never truly experience the power of God until you walk in the power of His love. Joseph cared! There countenance bothered him. What if Joseph thought to himself, *"Why bother? Why care? They deserve to be here I don't."* He would have missed his passage, his door out of prison.

Joseph worked the law of adaptability: Finally, the day came for his chance to be freed. Joseph, being a Hebrew and living and honoring his culture, made a decision to change his appearance in an effort not to offend the King. You see Egyptians were shaven people and Hebrew men were bearded men. Joseph understood that if he wanted to stay in the presence of Pharaoh he needed to at least appear to be pleasant to his sight. Getting an audience isn't the key, staying in the king's presence is.

> *"Then Pharaoh sent and called Joseph, and they brought*

him quickly out of the dungeon; and he shaved, changed his clothing, and came to Pharaoh." Genesis 41:14-15 NKJV

Do you see it? God used the storm, the rain, the wind and the flood to push this man to his future. I believe that we are promised the same outcome, if we do what God's people have done. Stay focused. Don't lose our praise.

Get ready you are about to experience RAIN!

Document Your Journey

TOPIC	THOUGHT

CHAPTER FOUR

FRESH BREAD

"Then said the LORD unto Moses, Behold, I will rain bread from heaven for you; and the people shall go out and gather a certain rate every day, that I may prove them, whether they will walk in my law, or no. And it shall come to pass, that on the sixth day they shall prepare that which they bring in; and it shall be twice as much as they gather daily." Exodus 16:4-5

~43~

DR. JERRY A. GRILLO, JR.

FRESH BREAD... AGAIN!

*T*he Children of Israel have, for some time, been on their journey to the promise land and God has taken them the long way. I've often wondered, why? I have since gotten my answer. God wanted to dry up all of the food that had been taken from Egypt.

God can't anoint and won't use a person who is still feeding themselves on the food from where they came from. You can't have one foot in Egypt and one foot on the promise. When we try to feast in both places, we become confused and disloyal. You can only serve one master. As long as the children of Israel could feed themselves and sustain themselves with the resources of Egypt, God wasn't going to advance them. Whatever is feeding you is what is sustaining you. Any move toward self sufficiency is a move away from God.

The two main resources we need to live are food and water. God allowed the children of Israel to run out of both. God wanted them to deplete all of their life sustaining resources from Egypt.

> *"And the children of Israel said unto them, Would to God we had died by the hand of the LORD in the land of Egypt, when we sat by the flesh pots, and when we did eat bread to the full; for ye have brought us forth into this wilderness, to kill this whole assembly with* **hunger.**" *Exodus 16:3*

Notice how they wanted the food of Egypt? They were craving it. That's how we are. The wilderness is necessary to stop us from loving our place of sin. God allows us the power of drought and loss so we will deplete all of our resources from Egypt... then and only then will we cry out for more food. Different food! Like babies wanting the bottle. Notice that God wasn't mad at them for wanting food, but immediately He had their answer. He was about to rain not water, but bread from heaven. You would think that God would have used the clouds to rain down water when they were thirsty and use the rocks for bread, but He does the complete opposite. He's always doing things differently than what the natural mind can comprehend.

Until you despise your present, your future will never materialize.

God allowed all of their food and water to dry up. When they became hungry, they cried out to God. Hunger is powerful. Hunger will drive you to satisfy a desire. We need to become hungry for God's food. You have to let go of the past if you want to grab hold of your future.

DON'T LIKE YOUR HARVEST? CHANGE YOUR SEED!

God desires for us to depend upon Him completely for our life sustaining power. If we do not, He's not going to share the one vital connection. It's okay to keep the wealth of Egypt, but not the life source of Egypt. The word '*depend*' gives us clarity as to why God is careful in not allowing those to advance in His promise, until they are totally dependant upon Him.

The word **"depend"** means to be influenced or determined by something else; to have trust; to rely on for support and aid from.

Our total focus must be on God. He is the source of all that sustains us. He is the power that moves us. It is in Him that we live, in Him that we move, and in Him that we have our being. (Acts 17:28)

When they ran out of water, God provided it from a rock...
When they ran out of food, God provided it from heaven...

WATER BEFORE BREAD:

Sequence matters to God. First water, then bread! The first substance that ran out was water. The first miracle after the Red Sea was turning bitter waters sweet. Before God can give you bread from heaven, He first has to deal with what has caused you to be bitter. Water represents the Spirit. The Spirit will come before the Bread. Bread represents the Word. Sequence matters. First, there must be a move of the Spirit before there can be revelation of the Word. God will not speak until He sees the Spirit present. The Spirit of the Lord was hovering over the face of the deep, then God spoke and said, "LET THERE BE..."

God has to deal with our internal before He deals with our external. Once this is finished, we can be ready for our eternal destination. Sequence matters! Internal... then external... for eternal provision... What's happening around us is a clue to what's going on in us. The internal world is more important than the external world. Focus on changing you; you will eventually change what's going on around you. If you don't like your harvest, change your seed!

Ambition is an attempt to succeed without God's intervention. The world has tapped into the power of humanism. They have learned how to use the resources around them to motivate them to succeed. But the truth is, that God doesn't want us to succeed void of His help. God wants us to believe Him for everything in our lives.

THE WILDERNESS IS NECESSARY:

Great men are not picked. Great men decide to be great. In reality, they pick themselves. People really don't pick their president; they pick a man who first decided to become the president. We don't call men out of the wilderness to lead us, we wait for them to come out of the wilderness then we follow. John the Baptist went into the wilderness, but when God was ready to lead men, Jesus came out of the wilderness to lead. There's something about the wilderness that qualifies men to lead. We lead only when we decide to come out. Jesus was led by the Holy Spirit to enter the wilderness (Mark 4), but it was his victories over the enemy that forced him out of the wilderness. It is in the dry, dead and weary place in our lives that train us... teach us... groom us... empty us...fill us. It is the wilderness where boys become men, students become teachers, weak becomes strong and fear turns into focus. It is after the wilderness experience that you become all that you've been called and destined to be.

Moses became the leader of his people after the wilderness of loss and sin. It was after Moses was exiled to the wilderness that he became who he was born to be, a deliver.

Joshua became Moses' replacement after forty years in the wilderness. It was in the wilderness that he learned how to fight, how to serve and how to lead. When he was ready to take the people through the Jordan and into something better, God led him out of the wilderness.

It wasn't until Elijah came out of the wilderness of loneliness, despair and depression that God anointed him to train and mentor a predecessor.

Right now you could be a person who is living in the dry place... a place in your home or marriage, even in your finances, where you feel you are left alone and surviving all by yourself. Maybe you're sensing right now that you are in a dead zone. A wilderness like you've never seen or heard about in all your life. I tell you this; you could be in a place where God is grooming you to be greater... more... even better than you used to be. Someone once asked me why I do what I do to help those who have failed and left for ruins. My answer is clear. I see the person they are and the person they are suppose to be. I believe that if I mentor and train, one day those two will meet and it should make for one great human being. I believe that once you see the man or woman you are suppose to be, you will never stay the man or woman you are. I believe in life after the wilderness. I believe that a bruised weed God will not despise or a smoldering wick he will not snuff out. Who are we to judge what God may be trying to fix? Who am I to write someone off that God has written in the book of greatness? I am going to die believing in the goodness of man. The wilderness is God's place... The wilderness is God's training ground for more... for better.

There will never be a day that I won't help someone who is reaching up for help. I'm not about exposing someone's weakness; they do that when they fall. I am about covering them to recovery; hiding them to be exalted later in the presence of God. I want to do what the blood of Jesus was assigned to do. Cover to cleanse... Cover to heal... Cover to promote. Hide to heal.

I preached a message years ago, *"If it dies, it multiplies."* My subtitle was, "Stop keeping alive what God has been trying to KILL!" The whole meaning of the message was that for something to live, something has to die. There has to be an exodus before there can be an entrance. You have to leave one place if you desire to enter the next place. Since we do not, as of yet, have glorified bodies, we can only be in one place at a time. God uses trials... God uses drought... God uses the devil... No matter how evil and how wicked the devil is, remember, he is still God's devil.

> **"STOP TRYING TO KEEP ALIVE WHAT GOD HAS BEEN TRYING TO KILL!"**

God uses the power of pain to push us to seek something greater for ourselves. This is exactly what happened when the Children of Israel cried out to God and God answered them. They went to bed hungry, but woke up the next morning with food all over the camp. During the night, during the dark times of hunger and pain, God answers with rain from heaven. This rain wasn't the rain of water, but the rain of bread. The Bible called it MANNA. Manna means *"What meaneth this?"* or better, "What is it?"

> *"Then said the LORD unto Moses, Behold, I will rain bread from heaven for you; and the people shall go out and gather a certain rate every day, that I may prove them, whether they will walk in my law, or no. And it*

shall come to pass, that on the sixth day they shall prepare that which they bring in; and it shall be twice as much as they gather daily." Exodus 16:4-5

Each day the command of the Lord was for the people to get up and gather enough "Manna" (bread) for the day. They were not to gather more than a one day supply. Daily, they were to get up in the morning and bend down low to gather the bread that was sent from heaven. Do you see the symbolism? God has a daily supply of revelation. Understand the sequence. The dew would fall, and then the bread (Manna) would be laid upon the dew. God would not lay His bread on the dirt, but on the dew. Remember, bread represents the Word, and the dew, or water, represents the Spirit. The dirt represents the flesh.

FLESH AND REVELATION DO NOT MIX:

Revelation without the Spirit is deadly. Revelation without wisdom is divisive. God will not place His Word of revelation on the flesh mind. He will always have a layer of the Spirit before He will impart His Words.

Notice, the only time they were to gather more than enough for one day was on the sixth day. They were to gather enough Manna to last for two days. I believe the Bible calls it "double." The people in the last days are supposed to be in position to receive a double portion. The rain of revelation that is about to fall, is going to increase us twice as much as any other generation. Let me go further.

I believe Joseph is a type of Christ. In the Bible, when Joseph was preparing to unveil his true identity to his brothers (the brothers are the representations of the ages), he sends his blessing and gives each brother a portion, but when Joseph gets to Benjamin, his youngest brother, the Bible says that he gave him five times as much. Five is the number of favor! I believe that Benjamin is sitting in the seat of the church age. I believe when Jesus defeated death and the grave and sat down at the right hand of the Father that He reached in His bowl of blessing and scooped out for the church the manna of power... the manna of double... the manna of Spirit... the manna of favor! God is trying to rain in our lives a double portion. Are you in position to receive the clouds of blessing?

> *"And they sat before him, the firstborn according to his birthright, and the youngest according to his youth: and the men marvelled one at another. And he took and sent messes unto them from before him: but Benjamin's mess was five times so much as any of theirs. And they drank, and were merry with him". Genesis 43:33-34*

The manna that was gathered on the sixth day had sustaining power attached to it. The manna that was gathered the day before would only last for a twenty-four hour period. God has placed in us an anointing by the Holy Spirit to sustain us.

MANNA ON US AND NOW MANNA IN US:

Manna, in the Hebrew means "What is it?" When the children of Israel got up that morning and looked out of their tents, they shouted "MANNA!" They shouted, "WHAT MEANTH THIS?" or, "WHAT IS IT?" It's bread from heaven. During the night it had rained. In the Old Testament, at best, the Holy Spirit would only perform acts on the people, or around them, but He would never enter in them. This was never God's full plan.

> *"And when the day of Pentecost was fully come, they were all with one accord in one place. And suddenly there came a sound from heaven as of a rushing mighty wind, and it filled all the house where they were sitting. And there appeared unto them cloven tongues like as of fire, and it sat upon each of them. And they were all filled with the Holy Ghost, and began to speak with other tongues, as the Spirit gave them utterance." Acts 2:1-4*

*"And they were all amazed, and were in doubt, saying one to another, **what meaneth this**"? Acts 2:12*

Do you see it? Can you understand it? They said the same thing. They shouted, "MANNA!" This manna wasn't going to rot in twenty-four hours. This manna was the bread of heaven falling into the hearts of men and women. This was the double portion. This was the most powerful rain ever to fall. It was the power to be filled with, instead of moved upon. *PRAY FOR RAIN!*

We are going to keep moving on in this book, but let's face it; right now there is enough to change your perspective. If you are one of those people who fight the Holy Spirit... **stop! Stop fighting the Holy Spirit**! Many fight Him because they have been told by someone that He doesn't do it that way anymore. Oh yeah? Who said? Why would you take the word of men instead of seeking the Truth from God? There is more to salvation than making heaven. There is being filled with God now! There is advancement to take place now. The Kingdom of possibility is now. My good friend, Pastor Terrell Murphy from New Birth Charlotte, ends his phone message with, *"Oh yeah, welcome to the age of possibility."* What does he mean by saying that? He means this, *"Welcome to the age of the Holy Spirit. Welcome to the age of being filled with the Kingdom."*

WHAT MEANETH THIS? GOD IN US! NOT GOD ON US

I understand there is a teaching that Jesus isn't coming back and that the *"rapture"* is never going to take place. I understand that the word "rapture" is not in the bible. I'm speaking of an exodus of the church. This doctrine that Christ isn't coming back to take his people away is wrong. Of course this is my opinion. Just because we preach that the Kingdom is now, doesn't mean that there won't be a Kingdom transfer. That transfer is going to be the entrance of the King! JESUS! READY or NOT, He's coming back! Just read the first chapter of the book of

Acts. "This same Jesus *will return* in like manner."

INTERNAL:
When Jesus came the first time, he came to regain the spirit. Man had been spiritually dead. Jesus died in our place, that through His death and resurrection He might revive the spirit of man. The Kingdom he set up was a Kingdom of dominion in the spiritual realm. When our spirit is connected to him, it becomes born again. To be born again you had to be born before. Some believe it's speaking of a second birthing that is after natural birth. Yes, it is a spiritual birth, but I don't believe it's second to natural birth. I believe that it refers to our spiritual renewal of what Adam gave up. Thus we are internally changed.

EXTERNAL:
When Jesus comes the second time, He is going to establish His external Kingdom. That external Kingdom is the people have been changed in a twinkling of an eye (raptured), will come back and rule with Him. That Kingdom will rule spiritually and physically. Yes, I believe that Jesus established His Kingdom when He came the first time, but I believe He only allows us to rule through His Spirit world first, but when He returns, and that return is close, He will set us up in both dimensions. Understand that we are comparing the two dimensions of rain, spiritual and physical rain. Just as the physical rain falls and has natural affects, so does the spiritual rain when it falls.

The rain falls because the soil has to be moistened for the seed to spring forth your harvest. The same is true for spiritual rain. The rain from Heaven falls on us that it might moisten our hearts, so that the seed of Jesus might spring forth. Then, what comes out of our mouths and attitudes is "manna," spiritual manna that is. This spiritual harvest is the product of the spiritual seed that has been sown in us. If there were no rain from Heaven, the seed would lay dormant. God wants us to position ourselves in His presence so that the spiritual "manna" can be reproduced in us and out of us to others who are hungry and don't know it. Those hungry for food, the kind of food that Jesus spoke of when He said that we have food the world knows not of.

FRESH BREAD!

Let me close this chapter with one more story. The famine had been so severe that it drove Naomi and her family out of the land of Bethlehem Judah. Famine is produced when the rains of heaven stop falling. Now, this famine had forced good people to seek help in a bad place. They moved to the land of the Moabites. The land of Moab was a land where the people did not seek the God of Naomi and her family. The only thing that Naomi learned in Moab was that her husband and sons died in the wrong place. I believe it would have been better for them to stay in the land of praise than to seek comfort in an ungodly land. Better to starve in God's presence than to be full in the wrong presence.

One day Naomi woke up in an ungodly city to hear the words of the messenger. **There is fresh bread in Bethlehem Judah again**. The famine was over. What happened? The heavens opened and the rain fell. When the rains fell, the land soaked it up and the seed began to grow, the flowers began to bloom, the trees began to sprout leaves, birds began to sing and the crops began to yield their harvest. When the rain falls, prosperity is the menu of the day.

Are you ready for the rain that produces Fresh Bread?

Document Your Journey

TOPIC	THOUGHT

CHAPTER FIVE

RAIN THAT FALLS IN DUE SEASON

"Then I will give you rain in due season, and the land
shall yield her increase... and their fruit."
Leviticus 26:4

RAIN THAT FALLS IN DUE SEASON

"Then I will give you rain in due season, and the land shall yield her increase, and the trees of the field shall yield their fruit." Leviticus 26:4

Due-season rain is rain that is appointed for the right time. Here we see another kind of rain. Seasonal rain!

How do we get to experience this due season of rain? We first have to follow the biblical pattern that is set up in verses one through three.

> *"Ye shall make you no idols nor graven image, neither rear you up a standing image, neither shall ye set up any image of stone in your land, to bow down unto it: for I am the LORD your God. Ye shall keep my sabbaths, and reverence my sanctuary: I am the LORD. If ye walk in my statutes, and keep my commandments, and do them;"* Leviticus 26:1-3

3 KEYS TO LIVE BY FOR POWERFUL RAIN:

1. Have no idols. What is idol worship? I've heard this when I was a teenage anything you go to in your hour of need becomes your God and it is an idol. Anything that is placed above or before the Lord is idol worship. *Have no sacred pillar or carved thing...* Is what God said. Many have made their television an idol. Don't tell me that your television isn't an idol in your house. Why does everything in the house face it? Do you spend more time looking at the TV than you do speaking to your children or spouse? Has your child ever come to you to ask you something and you were so engrossed in a television show that you chose to ignore them to finish watching your show? Think for a moment your favorite show is in reality a fantasy but that child was your reality. Now this isn't television bashing, it's just an observation.

Anything that rob's you of what God has designed for you could in the end be an idol.

2. Keep the Sabbath and reverence my sanctuary. This is probably one of the most disobeyed commands in the Bible. There are so many that call themselves Christians, who are not committed to a local church. The importance of church attendance has fallen off in this time and age. People once loved to gather and learn about the things of God. Now, we have become too busy. We have allowed our lives to be placed above the commands and wishes of God. I have talked to many pastors that have testified to the same thing. More than half of their congregation doesn't attend the mid-week services. My question is, why? Why do we allow things to keep us from gathering? Just let a major crisis hit and see if the church isn't packed the next week. We always need God when we are hurting. I believe it's time for us to raise the standard and place church and ministry above our own wants and desires. *"**Not forsaking the assembling of ourselves together**, as the manner of some is; but exhorting one another: and so much the more, as ye see the day approaching." {Hebrews 10:25}*

IT'S MY TIME FOR GOD'S FAVOR! IT'S MY TIME TO BE BLESSED!

We need to develop and train reverence again in the church. Reverence means to honor and to respect. Now, I don't know about you, but it seems that there is very little respect in the church. Respect for the carpet... the property... the walls.

Look around your church and watch how people are acting in the house of God.

3. *Walk in my statues and keep my commands...* This is not a suggestion; it's a command. These are God's laws. When we are in need of a miracle, it's the result of a law we have broken, thus, when we break God's laws, we are in need of a miracle.

YOU SHALL REAP IF YOU FAINT NOT:

"And let us not be weary in well doing: for in due season we shall reap, if we faint not. As we have therefore opportunity, let us do good unto all men, especially unto them who are of the household of faith." Galatians 6:9-10

The posture for reaping the benefits from the rain of blessing in due season is the position of not becoming weary in doing what is right. Let me encourage you; just because you haven't yet received your harvest, doesn't mean that you are not going to reap in due

Opposition is Opportunity in Disguise!

season. However long you've been waiting for your harvest may be a clue to how big your harvest is. Big movement requires more time!

Could it be taking more time to move things in their proper order - to rearrange things in your life and to prepare you for the posture to receive your due season harvest? Of course, God could certainly just speak a word and it would happen. It would appear immediately; however, the time it's been taking is for your benefit. God has added time to the equation for a proper harvest to manifest. We have to get involved with that harvest; people have to be positioned to receive the blessing.

CAPITALIZE ON OPPORTUNITY SWIFTLY:

God said in Galatians 6:9-10, *"As we have opportunity...;"* that opportunity is revealed in the verse, ***"let us do right unto all men."***

The word opportunity speaks to the moment in which we are facing crisis and circumstances. When we are under great weight because of crisis, delay or discouragement, it's easy to just want to throw up your arms and say, "Why continue?" What I'm trying to say is, don't get worn down because you have been forced into a posture of waiting. Refuse to allow the wait to force you to look and act differently in the moments of waiting. In these moments, God has hidden the key that will unlock your door of change and advancement. Opposition is opportunity in disguise. The Law of Hidden things! There is something hidden in the moment that the crisis is trying to mask so you can't see it. Those who wait on the Lord will renew their strength.

Let's discuss this word weary! First, we all have been beat down. We all have been stressed out because of delayed timing. Keep your focus... Keep your head up and your words positive. *Weary means to become fed up... tired... frustrated... angered... no more energy to try again.* Weary means that there will be a moment in your waiting when you may become weak; in those moments try not to miss your opportunity to do what is right. Engrafted in the crisis is the opportunity to excel. That's what God is trying to tell us through his servant Paul, that we are always in the right place to produce an outpouring of rain and blessing. Don't miss the opportunity to line up with God's laws.

When we are in line with God's laws... God is about to open the window of blessing and pour on us a due-season rain.

TWELVE BLESSINGS OF OBEDIENCE:

1. The land will yield its increase... Your seed is going to produce a major harvest.
2. Trees will yield its fruit.
3. The threshing floor shall be full with your harvest.
4. There will be peace. Your home will be a nest without thorns.
5. There will be no fear in your house. God will rid your life of evil intentions from others.

6. You will chase your enemy and your enemy shall flee from engaging against you.
7. God will look upon you favorably. He will cause you to be fruitful and multiply. To be fruitful, you first have to be seed full!
8. You will eat of the old harvest, and have to clear out the old for the new!
9. You will be respected by God.
10. God will accelerate your increase.
11. You will be set up in His presence and His presence will be set up around you.
12. God will destroy the yoke, and have you walking upright!

I don't know about you, but I'm going to walk in right standing with the Lord. I want to position myself for favor.

Reposition yourself for favor. Get in a place with God that causes the windows of Heaven to open. Right now start believing for your increase. Would you like to walk in a Deuteronomy 1:11 blessing?

1000 TIMES MORE:

I believe in these last days that we are not going to just experience a 100 fold return, but 1000 times more! Deuteronomy 1:11 says, *"...that you might increase 1000 times."* When this due-season rain falls, there will be such a powerful anointing on the rain that it will force the power within you and around you to increase 1000 times more. Would you like to experience 1000 times more? Then get ready for rain!

There is one more important qualifier to make this to happen.

You must be a tither. Malachi chapter three says that when we pay our tithes and sow our seeds, God will throw open the windows of Heaven. Some translations say, "The flood gates." God said He will pour out of those windows so much blessing that there will not be room enough for us to contain it. Now, that sounds like 1000 times more!

1000 times more pay... 1000 times more! It's yours if you activate the biblical code of believing, trusting and obeying God.

Tithe is not an exchange, it's an investment!

I understand the mentality of those who do not tithe... because it takes time to see it work. If you have been living for years ignoring the laws of God and then you start to obey them, you must place some time on the equation. Give God some time to work things in your favor. I call it the **LAW OF EVENTU-ALITY.**

Here's a challenge for you. Send the seed up... if it multiplies, its proof that God is there. (Mal. 3)

Once you understand that the tithe is not an exchange, but an investment, you will view it with different eyes. The sense of loss is traded for the excitement of increase. God promises that when we tithe and sow. God promises that he will open the windows of heaven and pour us out such a blessing there will not be room enough for it.

Giving is a powerful key that opens the windows of Heaven. Giving is the proof that you have conquered greed. Giving is the real proof of honor and love. The proof of God's love is that He sowed His gift of Jesus to us.

*"For God so loved the world, **that he gave** his only begotten Son, that whosoever believeth in him should not perish, but have everlasting life." John 3:16*

God so loved the world that He proved His love by giving. **"HE GAVE..."** I have a question for you. Did God give with a desired result? If your answer is yes, then here's another question. Is it wrong for us to give with a desired result? Some would say yes, but I believe the answer is no. It is not wrong for us to give or sow for a desired result. Seasonal rain is assigned to rain over our planted seeds. The tithe opens the window, but it is the seed that sits under that window that gives us the reason to have open windows from Heaven.

Let me give you one more reason that the tithe is an investment and not an exchange. For there to be an exchange, something has to be forfeited. In tithing and sowing, we have to learn that our giving is not an exchange but an investment.

Continually evaluate the return you receive from every investment you make. I'm not just speaking about money. I'm speaking about every investment you make in others, with your money and in time. Everything you invest in should bring you a return.

I can promise you that you will never invest in the Kingdom of God, that He won't bring you an awesome return.

Let me add here:

- *Stop investing in people who will not learn or change. Stop giving information to those who won't use it.*
- *Stop counseling people who will not listen.*
- *Move swiftly away from the nonproductive.*

Get serious about the laws of increase. A clean heart doesn't guarantee you a large bank account. Money is a magnifier. Money is a weapon. When a Christian has no money, they're missing one of their weapons. Satan has never feared a weaponless warrior.

FIVE THINGS THAT INTIMIDATE THE UNGODLY:

1. THE MASSES. When the Body of Christ starts growing, they begin to build voting power. The law of unity produces the glory. This promotes unity. For the masses to be affective, they will have to come into agreement to a vision, a project or a cause! Matthew 18:19 says that if any two of you agree on anything it

will be done... *(Paraphrased)*

2. WHEN MIRACLES OCCUR. The enemy cannot debate away a miracle. The enemy can debate the Gospel... he can debate a preacher...but there's no way he can debate a miracle. Miracles shut down the voice of the critic.

3. MONEY. Think for a moment. What if the people of God had plenty of money so that they could finance every project in the Kingdom of God? Wouldn't that be awesome? When the people of God have money, it makes the ungodly uncomfortable.

4. GOOD MARRIAGES! Marriage is focused ministry. Marriage is ministry at its highest level of excellence. If you violate another human being, you will violate God. Take care of your primary family, your marriage! There is no better power on the earth than a husband and wife who walk together in the unity of serving God.

5. PARENTS WHO LOVE GOD FIRST: This is the truth. When I was a youth pastor, I had more trouble with parents than I had with the devil. I would consistently have to talk to parents and train them to keep youth ministry a focus. Just when I got a young person loving youth service, the parents would get mad at their focus and love for the church. Guess what they would do? Ground them from youth service when the teenager did something wrong. Can you believe it? Don't ground your kids from the things of God. I tell you, the enemy hates parents who are sold out to God.

Document Your Journey

TOPIC	THOUGHT

CHAPTER SIX

THE PURPOSE FOR RAIN

"For as the rain comes down, and the snow from heaven,
And do not return there, **But water the earth***."*
Isaiah 55:10

THE PURPOSE FOR RAIN!

*"For as the rain comes down, and the snow from heaven, And do not return there, **But water the earth**, And make it bring forth and bud, That it may give seed to the sower And bread to the eater, So shall My word be that goes forth from My mouth; It shall not return to Me void, But it shall accomplish what I please, And it shall prosper in the thing for which I sent it." Isaiah 55:10-11*

*T*he first and natural reason for rain is to water the entire earth. Without rain, everything on the earth would eventually dry up and die. I love this passage in Isaiah 55, *"...the rain cometh and water the earth."* Why? Well let's break it down.

First, ***the rain brings forth bud***. In the spiritual, remember that water represents the Spirit. Bud means new growth. Without the bud on a tree, the tree will begin to lose its power of longevity. Buds are the youthfulness of the tree. Every spring we see the buds on plants that give it more beauty and life. Water produces the new growth, just as the rains from heaven in the spirit realm give the church new growth. I believe one of the reasons we see so few young people in church is because we have lost the clouds of rain in the Spirit. Our churches have become wastelands.

Secondly, ***rain gives seed to the sower***. I like this. God promises that if we sow, He will rain over our lives to give us seeds. For us to have seeds, we are going to have to experience a harvest. That's the reference of *'bread to the eater.'* When harvest comes, there will be a bountiful supply of food. Prosperity!

God compares this process with His words. Just as

the rain is gathered from the earth, it doesn't remain away from the earth for long. Whatever is taken from the earth is returned to the earth in storm clouds. The water on the earth is sown into the atmosphere and creates moisture, or weather changes. The water creates the cloud and the storm and the clouds travel to other parts of the earth to water what would otherwise die. The clouds that are created by the earth in one place create life in another place. This is how God's Word is. It is spoken from one place, so it can enter another place and sustain life. All of this is in the rains of heaven. Look at this word process.

God's word leaves His mouth and it must enter someone's ear. Romans chapter ten says, *"Faith comes by hearing and hearing by the Word of God."* When the Word of God is received, it creates energy of faith. It destroys the fear of failure and the worry of defeat. God's Word produces a cloud of focus and we become pregnant with a seed.

After you've digested the truth, you will become God's cloud, and He will carry you to a wasteland of people who are in need of rain. God's rain... God's Word! When you open your mouth, you will return unto Him through the ears of others, God's words. So the Words of God did not return unto Him void. They went out and accomplished all He sent them out to do. The natural rain is produced when a cloud opens up and leaks what is in them. So it is with the spiritual rain, when we open our mouths and let out what is in us.

Now, if we are wounded... if we haven't dealt with past pains and failures, then what leaks out of our mouths is not the Words of God, but the poisons of our wounds... Can bitter waters and fresh waters co-exist in the same well? No!

God's Word, in this dimension, is sent out from the Word of God (Bible) and enters our hearts to change our way of thinking... to motivate us to be like Him (Jesus). After we have incubated that Word, it comes out of our belly as a well of living water. Where did that water come from? It came from the rain of heaven.

"He that believeth on me, as the scripture hath said, out of his belly shall flow rivers of living water." John 7:38

THE WORD WITHIN US:

I once heard someone say, *"Once upon a time, in time, when there was no time, in a place called nowhere, there was a meeting. In that meeting, the Lamb was slain, and resurrected, and the enemy was defeated. Present in that meeting were God the Father, God the Son (Jesus), God the Holy Spirit and you. You were in that meeting before time began. Before the foundations of the world, God knew you."*

DIVINE MOMENTS ARE RELEASED WHEN WE ARE ON A DIVINE MISSION

*"According as he hath chosen us in him **before the foundation of the world**, that we should be holy and without blame before him in love" Ephesians 1:4*

*"Who verily was **foreordained before the foundation** of the world, but was manifest in these last times for you." 1 Peter 1:20*

Just a thought! Could it be that everything we've gone through here on the earth was something we may have agreed to in that meeting before time?

"But we have this treasure in earthen vessels, that the excellency of the power may be of God, and not of us." 2 Corinthians 4:7

God placed in us His seed and that seed is His Word. The English language teaches us that you must have a noun and a verb to make a complete sentence. A word by itself has no meaning. Each of us is a Word spoken in that place before time.

To make it clearer, call that "Word" our purpose, our assignment. We have no power alone. Alone we have no meaning.

LAW OF TWO:

When a verb is attached to a noun it gives that noun meaning. The verb causes action to be ascribed to the noun. *Example: I came. I saw. I conquered. Jesus wept. She ran. He loved.* When the verb is attached to the noun it gives the noun purpose... meaning. This is the best example I can give to describe the power of connection, the law of two. The Bible says that five of us can chase a hundred, and a hundred can chase ten-thousand. The number of increase is ten thousand times stronger.

> *"And five of you shall chase an hundred, and an hundred of you shall put ten thousand to flight: and your enemies shall fall before you by the sword." Leviticus 26:8*

AGREEMENT UNLOCKS THE OIL

Unity is the greatest asset to advancing the Kingdom. For the rain to fall from heaven there has to be unity in the land. The power of agreement releases the oil that unlocks the clouds that causes the rain from heaven to fall.

> *"Again I say unto you, That if two of you shall agree on earth as touching any thing that they shall ask, it shall be done for them of my Father which is in heaven. For where two or three are gathered together in my name, there am I in the midst of them." Matthew 18:19-20*

Think for moment about what I am saying. If you were the enemy and you had this understanding, what would you do to prevent the Kingdom's advancement? Would it be division? The spirit of division is the strongest weapon the enemy has to destroy our churches and dam up the heavens. Many of us are sitting under closed heavens because we have caused division in God's house.

Just look around. Drive around your city and see how many churches there are. So many small, do nothing places. These places were started by the spirit of offense, pride or just plain disobedience with no spiritual covering or power to exist. They are ministries, if you can call them that, with no identity, illegitimate in origin. The word illegitimate means you've been born out of an act of lust, and the two have not agreed to come into covenant. Thus, the result is a child born with no last name or without the last name of the father. This causes what was born out of wedlock to be called illegitimate. So many ministries are out of order. They have been tagged by God as illegitimate because they caused division and left to birth what they were not sanctioned to do.

The purpose of people is to experience the rain of heaven and allow that rain to cause the harvest of God to increase in them. God's seed in us is waiting on the rain and that seed is the treasure of God; His word, placed in us before the foundation of the world. We are nothing but soil and when the rain falls on us, the seed that was planted in us grows!

Each of us has a specific assignment. One of us could be the noun, others are the verbs and some could be adjectives, pronouns, etc. When we are locked up together, we create sentences, sentences create paragraphs, and paragraphs create stories.

Alignment:

God is waiting for us to get in alignment to His Word. Alignment is the positioning of something for proper performance. When we are in alignment to God's Word, which is the Word of God spoken in us, that spoken word will align itself to the written Word in the Bible, and then the power of the Word is released.

When we are out of alignment, we begin to operate like a car that is out of alignment. If your car is not aligned properly, the car tends to always veer off course. If you are not completely alert, you will eventually run off the road, possibly wreck and cause harm to yourself, as well as others. Misalignment will also cause your tires to wear out prematurely.

The same is true with us. When we are out of alignment to God's plan and purpose for our lives, we will spend more time doing but going nowhere. Our life wears out sooner. We become tired... we become depressed... we become angry and a sense of uselessness is birthed in us. As a result, we spend most of our time trying to fix ourselves. Doctors, lawyers, and counselors... We become the woman who had an issue of blood for twelve years. After she spent all she had on physicians, she grew worse. But when she finally got to Jesus, she was made whole. When she aligned her faith to His will, she was delivered. Did you get that? She positioned herself in the proper place for God to rain healing down on her life. Let me give you one more definition to alignment. *The correct position or positioning of different components relative to one another, so that they perform properly...*

THE ALIGNMENT OF YOUR ASSIGNMENT PRODUCES YOUR ADVANCEMENT!

Assignment:

Your alignment creates an understanding of your assignment. It is in the rain of heaven that God has scheduled your provision. That provision is attached to your assignment. Finances are not following you, they are waiting on you. Money and provision are sitting in the place you are assigned to be. Dr. Mike Murdock, my mentor, said to me, *"You can't create your assignment, you can only discover it."*

When your spirit is lined up with God's Spirit, God will begin to give you clarity as to what you are assigned to do. When you are fulfilling your God given assignment, Heaven will open and God will begin to pour out on you the latter and former day rain. To seize a divine moment, you must discover your divine mission. Not everyone's assignment is to preach from a pulpit or to do a television ministry. Everybody can't be the head, but all of us can discover our purpose and assignment. Some may be workers, others intercessors, evangelists, missionaries and some may just keep the church clean. I heard a song once and the phrase that keeps ringing in my mind right now is, *"If just a cup of water I place within your hands, then just a cup of water is all that I will demand..."* That's it? That's it! This should be enough to make the point clear.

When we are doing what we have been sent here to do, competition will stop. Jealousy and envy in the church will cease. Hatred and bitterness will become a thing of the past. Love will be the most powerful weapon in the house of God, and the heavens will open and the rain of heaven will fall!

Advancement:

When the rain falls, we will begin to advance again. We will take new territories. We will take our cities, then our states, and once again, we will reclaim our country. This is the purpose for the rain. Pray for rain right now. Ask the Lord to send the rain; to open the windows of Heaven and let it pour. Pour over your finances... let it pour over your mind... let it pour over your home and family... Why don't you just lift your hands and let the heavens open. Let God wash over your life.

Connection:

Connection decides agreement. When you hook up with someone, you are making a covenant with that person. This covenant could be a partnership of failure and not success. The enemy is looking for a door to destroy you everyday. Be very laborious in deciding who you connect to. Be very cautious who you eat with in public. I heard a story one time that illustrates this very well.

This preacher was teaching another young minister in his town about the law of association. He told him whatever you do, don't sit down in public and eat with those you know are living in habitual sins. Let say a person is living in in adultery. You decide to eat with him in public. Someone will walk by the restaurant and say to the other person they are with; **one of those men sitting there is an adulterous person, I can't remember which one.** *Now you are tagged with the sin of another. Bad company can corrupt good morals.*

What you connect to, you will eventually become. Whatever you do, don't ignore this law. The kind of rain you could be experiencing right now may be the result of the connections you've decided to make. Make good connections.

Document Your Journey

TOPIC	THOUGHT

CHAPTER SEVEN

ACTIONS THAT CAN CAUSE THE ABSENCE OF RAIN

DR. JERRY A. GRILLO, JR.

DECISIONS THAT CAUSE THE ABSENCE OF RAIN

*W*hen God withholds the rain, it could be because there is something in the land that has caused His anger to kindle.

> *"When heaven is shut up, and there **is no rain**, because they have sinned against thee; if they pray toward this place, and confess thy name, and turn from their sin, when thou afflictest them: Then hear thou in heaven, and forgive the sin of thy servants, and of thy people Israel, that thou teach them the good way wherein they should walk, and **give rain upon thy land**, which thou hast given to thy people for an inheritance." 1 Kings 8:35-36*

The first reason God withholds the rain from heaven is because we have sinned against Him. This scripture in I Kings is speaking about natural rain, but in the New Testament there is a transition to spiritual rain; which is the presence of the Lord.

SERVING OTHER GODS WILL CAUSE THE HEAVENS TO SHUT UP:
> *"Take heed to yourselves, lest your heart be deceived, and you turn aside and serve **other gods and worship them**, lest the LORD's anger be aroused against you, and He shut up the heavens **so that there be no rain**,*

*and the land yield no produce, and you perish quickly
from the good land which the LORD is giving you."
Deuteronomy 11:15-17 NKJV*

Idol Worship is any object that is greatly and often
fanatically admired and loved. Worship is when we add worth to
something. An idol doesn't necessarily have to be something you
call God; however, an idol can be anything we love and admire
more than God. For example, **your television could be an
idol.** Your job, money, even you could be an idol.

OUR CHILDREN CAN BE AN IDOL... I've witnessed many parents
who have placed their children's activities before the activities of
God.

OUR FAVORITE SPORTS TEAM CAN BE AN IDOL... I know of
people who won't come to church on a given Sunday because
their team is playing and kick off starts before they can get home.
What a shame.

YOUR CAREER CAN BE AN IDOL, especially when it is more
important than God's principles. People will compromise their
principles to make sure that they can get the next promotion. I
have often told businessmen to make sure that they check out the
churches in the area where they are planning to move. Don't
become fixated on an increase of money if you have to weaken
your walk with God to get it.

CHURCH AND DENOMINATION CAN BECOME AN IDOL and hinder
the rain from heaven. Many have lost the presence of God simply
because they choose to stay in a dead place. Why? Why do people
trade God out? I don't know! I've seen some pretty wicked things
done in the name of Christ. I've heard of deacon boards throwing
pastors out; congregations dividing and warring against each
other over stupid things. I was once a youth pastor in a church
where I was voted in by the deacon Board. After a few months,

the youth group starting growing and becoming multicultural. Guess what happened next? You guessed it. I was fired. Well, I was asked to resign. When I asked why, their answer was mean and racist. I can tell you to this day, God isn't moving in that church. The rain has been withheld. Instead of allowing God to be God and aligning themselves with His Word, they chose to make their building and their stuff their god. Let me ask you a question. Does God love our property more than He loves His people?

MONEY CAN BE AN IDOL... We will spend forty plus hours a week of our best time working for money, and become angry if church is more than two hours long once a week. You tell me if your money is your god. If not, then why is it so hard to let it go? When your pastor asks for a money offering, why do we tend to negotiate with God on how much we should give?

The trick of idol worship is that we deceive ourselves. We say we don't love things, yet, there is always something keeping us from fulfilling our divine purpose. We are no better than the children of Israel when they built the golden calf. All we've done is make a different calf. Hear me, anything we show more love to than God could be an idol in the eyes of the Lord.

LACK OF INTEREST IN THE HOUSE OF GOD:

> *"When I shut up heaven and there is no rain, or command the locusts to devour the land, or send pestilence among My people, if My people who are called by My name will humble themselves, and pray and seek My face, and turn from their wicked ways, then I will hear from heaven, and will forgive their sin and heal their land. Now My eyes will be open and My ears attentive to prayer made in this place. For now I have chosen and sanctified this house, that My name may be there forever; and My eyes and My heart will be there perpetually. As for you, if you walk before Me as your*

father David walked, and do according to all that I have commanded you, and if you keep My statutes and My judgments, then I will establish the throne of your kingdom, as I covenanted with David your father, saying, 'You shall never fail to have a man as ruler in Israel." 2 Chronicles 7:13-18 NKJV

There is such a frivolous attitude today in the house of God. People are not making God's house and the gathering of God's people a priority any more. We would rather stay home and cut our grass and manicure our lawns than come to church.

IF GOD DOESN'T HEAR OUR PRAYER THEN SATAN IS NOT OBLIGATED TO HEAR OUR REBUKES!

Someone once said, "You don't have to go to church to be a Christian." I beg to differ. If that person is truly what they say they are, a *Christian*, then wouldn't it be safe to say that church would be a priority? **Of course it would**! Your focus on the house of God determines God's focus on your house.

*"Then the word of the LORD came by Haggai the prophet, saying, "Is it time for you yourselves to dwell in your paneled houses, and this temple to lie in ruins?" Now therefore, thus says the LORD of hosts: **"Consider your ways!** "You have sown much, and bring in little; You eat, but do not have enough; You drink, but you are not filled with drink; You clothe yourselves, but no one is warm; And he who earns wages, Earns wages to put into a bag with holes. Thus says the LORD of hosts: **"Consider your ways!** Go up to the mountains and bring wood and build the temple, that I may take pleasure in it and be glorified," says the LORD. You looked for much, but indeed it came to little; and when you brought it home, I blew it away. Why?" says the LORD of hosts. **"Because of My house that is in***

ruins, while every one of you runs to his own house. Therefore __the heavens above you withhold the dew, and the earth withholds its fruit.__ For I called for a drought on the land and the mountains, on the grain and the new wine and the oil, on whatever the ground brings forth, on men and livestock, and on all the labor of your hands." Haggai 1:3-11 NKJV

Did you notice we work much, but bring home little? There are holes in our sacks and those holes aren't caused by the devil, they are caused by our lack of interest in God's house. God is cutting those holes! Place God's house and His work as a priority on your list and watch the heavens open and the rain of His blessings come down.

WRONG GROWTH IN GOD'S HOUSE WILL STOP THE RAIN OF HIS PRESENCE.

"And now, O inhabitants of Jerusalem and men of Judah, Judge, please, between Me and My vineyard. What more could have been done to My vineyard That I have not done in it? Why then, when I expected it to bring forth good grapes, Did it bring forth wild grapes? And now, please let Me tell you what I will do to My vineyard: I will take away its hedge, and it shall be burned; And break down its wall, and it shall be trampled down. I will lay it waste; It shall not be pruned or dug, But there shall come up briers and thorns. I will also command the clouds that __they rain no rain on it__." Isaiah 5:3-6 NKJV

The word *vineyard* is a type and shadow of God's people. Can bitter waters and fresh waters dwell in the same well? No! God is concerned as to why His children, or vineyard, have grown up to be wild grapes. He expected the people that were saved to grow up and be like Him. He wanted us to walk in love and to possess the spirit of graciousness instead of being wild and rebellious. The lack of spiritual mentorship is costing us dearly.

Seeker-safe mentality is not, in my opinion, helping the body of Christ. If anything, it is teaching us to be **offense sensitive.** One of the greatest problems in the church today is the lack of being able to correct anyone. Correction is the proof of connection. If you can't be corrected, you can't be connected. One of my staff members once asked me why I was always correcting them. My answer was, "The day I stop correcting you, your future no longer matters to me."

To build a healthy family there has to be the willingness by the parent to discipline, to correct when there have been infractions in the house. When the rules are broken, there has to be consequences. In this, we teach our children manners and respect. Look around at the teenagers today. Have you noticed how disrespectful they are to adults? Why? No one is able to correct them anymore. When I went to school, the teacher was able to place a paddle on your backside. I can tell you this; it wouldn't take too many of those pops on the backside for our teenagers to straighten up. When there is a lack of discipline in the church, it causes people to mature in a rebellious and wrong way.

SEEKER SENSITIVE IS REALLY TEACHING US HOW TO BE "OFFENSE SENSITIVE"!

Every time you turn around someone in the church is offended. The biggest lie of Satan is the lie of hurt feelings. When did God ever concern Himself with the feelings of others when it came to telling the truth? I fear if Jesus were trying to pastor in America, He would be voted out in the next business meeting.

WHEN WE TRUST IN MAN'S WAYS AND IGNORE GOD'S WAYS, THE RAIN WILL STOP COMING.

"Because the ground is parched, For there was no rain in the land, The plowmen were ashamed" Jeremiah 14:4 NKJV

"Because you have forgotten me and trusted in falsehood." Jeremiah 13:25NKJV

"I have seen your adulteries and your lustful neighing, the lewdness of your harlotry, your abominations on the hills in the fields. Woe to you, O Jerusalem!" Jeremiah 13:27 NKJV

Trust is important to God. The proof of faith is trust. Faith believes God can, trust believes God will. By faith, step out on what He said He can do.

FAITH BELIEVES GOD CAN...TRUST BELIEVES GOD WILL!

Worry is confidence in your adversary... Faith is confidence in God. Fear is the currency of hell. Faith is the currency Heaven flows in. When we are trusting in man's ability, we are voiding out the power and ability of God. I say, some trust in chariots... some trust in horses... I will trust in the Name of the Lord! When we stop trusting God and start worrying, we stop the rain of His presence from falling.

AN ANGRY COUNTENANCE AND A BACKBITING TONGUE CAN STOP THE RAINS FROM COMING:

"The north wind driveth away rain: so doth an angry countenance, a backbiting tongue." Proverbs 25:23

Countenance matters to God. Let me show you how powerful your countenance is.

"So the LORD said to Cain, "Why are you angry? And why has your countenance fallen? If you do well, will you not be accepted? And if you do not do well, sin lies at the door. And

~89~

*its desire is for you, but you should rule over it." Genesis 4:6-8
NKJV*

God was observing things on the earth and noticed that
Cain wasn't doing very well. How does God know this? Cain's
countenance exposed him. God asks Cain, *"Why has your
countenance fallen?"* The reason was because he was angry with
his brother, Abel. His brother had offered a sacrifice to God, so
Cain decided to do the same. The problem began when God
accepted Abel's sacrifice and rejected Cain's. Cain became so
angry and his anger turned into jealousy, which then affected his
countenance.

What gets my attention is what God says to Cain. *"...Sin
lies at the door, and its desire is for you, but you should rule
over it (Him)."* The word *sin,* in the Hebrew is translated from
the phrase, "Man of sin." This wasn't just an act that was lying at
the door of Cain's life, it was Lucifer. The enemy was causing
Cain to become angry by feeding his mind with thoughts of
jealousy and envy. Wrath is cruel, anger is outrageous, but who
can stand against envy? God informs Cain that he should rule
over him!

Let me ask a question. How can a man in the Old
Testament rule over Satan? This is before Christ. This is before
the cross and the resurrection. This is a time when men lived
under the attack and dominion of the enemy; yet, God let's us in
on a secret. Cain *could* rule the man of sin, the enemy. Cain could
do this with his COUNTENANCE! Our countenance is strong!

Countenance is the look or expression on one's face that
shows one's nature or feelings. How can our countenance rule?
When your countenance is protected, you stop the enemy from
picking up valuable information. The way we look, the expression
of anger, is feeding information to the enemy that what he is
doing is working. The circumstance he has chosen to surround
you with is getting your focus... your attention. Thus, the enemy
knows that it's just a matter of time before you will cave in, give
in and fall. If Cain would have gotten control of his countenance,

he could have ruled over the enemy. An angry countenance drives away the rains of blessing.

SOME FACTS ABOUT COUNTENANCE:

- Your countenance is louder than your voice.
- Countenance enters the room before you do.
- Your countenance can change the atmosphere and stop a miracle.
- Your countenance lets others know what you are feeling.
- Your countenance is giving away valuable information.
- Countenance is the expression of your attitude.
- Countenance can destroy your access, or facilitate it.
- Your countenance can hinder others.
- Countenance matters to God.
- Countenance has a presence.

The word *countenance* appears fifty-three times in the King James Version. God is watching our countenance. Our friends are watching our countenance and so is the enemy. Your countenance could be affecting your ability to experience the rains of heaven.

DR. JERRY A. GRILLO, JR.

CHAPTER EIGHT

PROCESS TO INCREASE

*"Elijah said unto Elisha, Ask what I shall do for thee, before I be taken away from thee. And Elisha said, I pray thee, **let a double portion** of thy spirit be upon me..." 2 Kings 2:9*

PROCESS FOR A DOUBLE PORTION

"And the LORD restored Job's losses when he prayed for his friends. Indeed the LORD gave Job **twice as much** *as he had before." Job 42:10 NKJV*

STEP ONE: SEASON OF CONFRONTATION:

You can never enter the next season unless you are willing to confront what is holding you in your present season. You can never change what you are unwilling to confront.

Many never leave their present because they have accepted their life and lifestyle.

You can't win wars by evacuation; you win wars by confrontation. Confrontation is the ability to stand up and fight for what is right. It is the force that will create change in your world.

> **YOU DON'T WIN WARS BY EVACUATION, YOU WIN THEM BY CONFRONTATION!**

Confrontation means to stand up and face boldly and defiantly.

I believe that the church has entered a season where we have become too passive in our stand for Godly things. This seeker sensitive mentality is not biblical. What we are doing isn't training people to stand up and speak out, but to sit and hide in the four walls of religion. The seeker-safe mentality is weakening the church. This philosophy is not developing better warriors, but **"offense sensitive"** Christians.

REFUGEE CAMPS

This evacuation mentality is causing us to build refugee camps. A refugee is someone who flees from home, or country, to seek refuge elsewhere; as in times of war, or political and religious persecution. A refugee is someone who isn't willing to die for what they believe. God hasn't called us to be refugees; He's called us to take up the amour of God and fight. We are to fight the good fight of faith. We are not of those who shrink back, but we are of those who stand in times of persecution and fight!

We must confront the issues that are in and around our lives, if we desire to move on to the next level with God. You can't fix what you are unwilling to face.

Opposition is a hidden doorway to opportunity.

Stand up and fight! If you have addictions, fight them! If you are under attack in your mind, then fight those wrong thoughts! If you have marital problems, fight for your marriage! Divorce is not the answer. The answer is confrontation! If you desire double, then prepare for war!

STEP TWO: SEASON OF ACCELERATION:

WITHOUT FEAR THERE WOULD BE NO REASON FOR COURAGE

This is the place where God starts to ease up the crisis. This is the season where increase begins to enter your life. When the mist, so to speak, is placed on the ground of your life and you will begin to feel God and sense God.

This season is very important. It is in this time that God sets a hedge about you, and gives you time to build your information pool about Him and to feel Him in your praise and worship. When you're in this season, you must eat and drink as much as you can. Take this time to refresh your mind and equip your spirit. This time won't last forever.

Here, if we are not careful, we will become religious. This is where mediocrity sets in. We will assume, because there is a time of peace; that we have arrived. This is not the harvest; this is just a resting place for God to build your faith.

This is the season where God, through His Word, begins to align us to His purpose. Here is where things begin to fall off of our lives and out of our minds, and we begin to develop the mind of God. **Alignment creates your assignment!**

If we're not careful, we will begin to develop a religious mindset in this season. Remember, this season is only for a moment. This is only the process of preparing you and equipping you for something bigger.

This is the season when the child starts to turn into a son. When did Jesus stop being God's child and start being His Son? He stopped being the child when He came into alignment to God's purpose!

STEP THREE: SEASON OF FRUSTRATION:

When God gives you a promise, a season of delay is attached to it. A delayed promise causes us to become frustrated.

Life is anointed to frustrate you. What makes this a harder thing to swallow is when your frustrations are being led by God. God is allowing this season to force the real you to surface. This season is hard. This season comes right after a major victory. After the season of acceleration, prepare for a season of frustration and delay.

THINGS THAT CAN PRODUCE A FRUSTRATED MIND:

1. **Delayed Promises:** When promises or your harvest don't come when you expect it to, this can cause a glitch in the mind that may cause you to think that your promise isn't coming. This mind set begins to create worry. Worry is confidence in the adversary.

2. **Discouragement:** When your promise is delayed, you can begin to enter into a season of discouragement. Look at the word discouragement when it is broken up; "dis" and "courage." Discouragement will cause you to lose the courage to believe, to stand and to fight. It takes courage to call order to chaos. Discouragement can develop an inadequate mind set. Your identity begins to come into question and disappointment begins to birth.

3. **Disappointment:** This stage produces the downward spiral to the end. Disappointment is when expectation is not fulfilled. Have you ever felt disappointed? What happened to your faith at that moment? It was dying!

4. **Depression:** This is usually the result of being disappointed. Depression can start out minor, but I believe that if it is not confronted immediately it can turn into a spirit.

5. **Distraction:** Distractions will change your focus. Focus reveals what you believe. Focus decides direction. The battle for your life is over your focus. Focus is what the mind decides to concentrate on. Focus is what the mind becomes obsessed over. Focus will decide what you feel. What you feel determines what you will pursue.

    Now, the mind is becoming persuaded that victory is not possible. Most people are locked into their own perception. Defeat is inevitable. You are becoming what you keep looking at. Someone once said to me that "what you keep looking at will master you."

    Why are so many still broke? All they keep looking at is debt. Why do so many stay sick? Because all they keep talking about is their pain... there sickness. This formula works for most every situation in your life.

6. **Defeat:** The enemy has you right where he wants you; convinced that there is no way out. Persuaded to accept your life instead of fighting everyday to change your life. People who stop changing become defeated. Ignorance is the refusal to change.

Faith is a decision of the mind that forces everything else to line up to it.

To survive this season of frustration, first and foremost, you must not allow a spirit of discouragement to enter your emotions. To be discouraged is to be without courage. This doesn't mean that in a season of loss or bad news, that you don't experience fear. Fear will never leave us. Without fear, courage wouldn't be necessary. Courage finds its meaning through fear. Courage is moving on even when we are experiencing fear. When we allow our frustrations to control us, we allow discouragement and disappointment to own us. When we place too much emphasis on those around us and they fail to live up to our expectations, we become disappointed. Disappointment is proof that we are focusing too much on the external world and not enough on the Christ that lives in us.

If Satan distracts you, he has you. Whatever you are focusing on is mastering you. If your attention and focus is on the loss that is around you; guess what? That's all you will attract.

Depression is a deadly weapon of frustration.

Depression stops us from pressing forward, from believing that there is hope. When someone is considering taking their own life, it is usually because they have lost hope.

For us to succeed in walking in the season of blessing and increase, we are going to have to survive this major season. Many have fallen short of the greatest seasons for their life simply because they could not pass the season of frustration.

IT TAKES COURAGE TO CALL ORDER TO CHAOS

This is the qualifying stage. You must pass this stage. It is in this season when God begins to press out of you what doesn't belong in you. You are in the greatest and most dangerous season when you're in the season of frustration. You can move forward and believe for what is coming next, or you can succumb to the weight and crumble and fall.

This is the place where conception takes place...

Here is where God births your Isaac. It's right here in this season that God births your real ministry. Here is where God begins to speak to you about what's coming. This season, is the season that separates the real from the counterfeit.

STEP FOUR: SEASON OF SEPARATION:

Frustration produces separation...

Not everybody in your life belongs in your life. Sometimes God holds back all of the promise and blessing because someone is connected to us that does not belong. Those who don't qualify for your harvest could be holding up your blessing. Separation births the greatest season for our lives. Too much flesh hinders promised pregnancy.

STEP FIVE: SEASON OF MULTIPLICATION:

Man hoards, Satan subtracts but God multiplies. The fastest way to increase is when God places the anointing of multiplication on your life. This is where the double portion power lives. It lives in the process of survival. It lives in the ability to stay connected when others are leaving, giving God time to schedule a season of promotion and blessing for you. You will never qualify for this stage and blessing if you don't pass through all the other stages.

The safest place to be is the next place. Don't get stuck in one season, especially the season of acceleration. Open up your faith and allow God the privilege of moving you through all five seasons. Trust me, you want to experience the season of multiplication.

This is the place where the former and latter day rains mingle together. (Joel 2:23) This is the season where you no longer have to glean the field, but you now own the field. It is at this place, where you move from being the one who is always in need; to being the one who is meeting the needs of others. WOW! What a place to be!

Document Your Journey

TOPIC	THOUGHT

CHAPTER NINE

NO WORSHIP...
NO RAIN!

*"And it shall be that whichever of the families of the earth
do not come up to Jerusalem to worship the King, the
LORD of hosts, on them there **will be no rain**. If the
family of Egypt will not come up and enter in, they shall
have no rain"*
Zechariah 14:17-18 NKJV

NO WORSHIP NO RAIN

*T*his one is my favorite versus. I preached a whole series on this one phrase, **NO WORSHIP NO RAIN.** Worship is so misunderstood in church. We really believe that worship is singing slow songs and lifting up our hands at the same time. The truth is, that many in our congregations who lift their hands and sing, are not really worshipping. The reason I say this is, because for us to worship, there has to be a recipient of that worship. Someone has to receive what we are offering up.

> *"Who shall ascend into the hill of the LORD? or who shall stand in his holy place? He that hath clean hands, and a pure heart; who hath not lifted up his soul unto vanity, nor sworn deceitfully." Psalm 24:3-4*

That should be clear! When we lift our dirty, unforgiving hands, God is not receiving anything from us. If we have alt with our brothers and sisters in the Lord, God said that He wouldn't even hear our prayers, much less, receive our worship. If God doesn't hear our prayers, then Satan isn't obligated to hear our rebukes.

Worship is acquisition. Worship places us in position for the rain of heaven to pour. Worship is the attitude of people who are willing to become pregnant with God's seed. Spiritual conception takes place in worship. Worship opens Heaven's resources and no worship shuts them up. Each week in churches all over people refuse to really enter into worship. They sing a few songs, but when the Spirit starts to enter... when He's about to pour out the spiritual rain in the place... the order of service is changed.

THE QUICKEST WAY INTO GOD'S PRESENCE IS THROUGH SINGING PRAISES

Praise is good, but worship is better. Everyone must and can praise God. The sinner is allowed to praise Him. The Bible says, *"Let everything that has breath, praise the Lord."* The pattern of the Old Testament was that everyone was allowed in the outer court. Thus, everyone was allowed to shout to the Lord, but only the priest was allowed to move deeper into the heart and presence of God.

- *Praise enjoys God, but worship esteems Him*
- *Praise acclaims God, but worship beholds Him.*
- *Praise lifts God, but worship bows to Him.*
- *Praise affirms God, but worship loves Him.*
- *Praise addresses God, but worship waits on Him.*
- *Praise dances, but worship lays at His feet.*
- *Praise extols God for what He has done, but worship extols Him for who He is.*
- *Praise sings about God, worship sings to God.*
- *Praise sings about their crowns, worshippers lay their crowns at His feet. Author Unknown*

In our local denominations, we have become bias on what real worship is. I can tell you for sure what it is not. It's not singing three or four songs and quickly moving on in the order of the service so that we can exit the people at a certain time. ***Real worship is unrehearsed.*** Real worship can't be placed on a time contingent. We have reduced our weekly services into a mindset of, "let's get it done quickly." Our personal lives have become our focus; not God's presence and voice.

The proof that there has been no rain is that the ground is parched and dried up. Look around, take a close evaluation of the people in your local congregation, do they look dried up?

"Because the ground is parched, for there was no rain in the land, the plowmen were ashamed; they covered their heads." Jeremiah 14:4 NKJV

Refusal to offer up the right kind of worship causes God to not open up the windows of heaven and rain upon us His presence and blessing. I can't imagine living under a closed heaven. I want to open my hands and worship, so that God may open His hand and cover me with His power and love. Living under an open heaven gives us the rain that is necessary to have a wonderful life. When God rains over our finances, they grow. When He rains over our marriage, it grows in love and peace. God's spiritual rain in our churches will cause our congregations to grow. We need the rain from heaven!

The proof of worship is pursuit. The teaching in our churches about *waiting* has destroyed the doctrine of pursuit. People are just sitting around waiting for God to do something. Noah didn't sit around waiting for his ship to come in... he built his! I know what you're thinking, *"But the Bible says, 'they that wait on the Lord shall renew their strength'."* Yes, it does say that in *Isaiah 40: 31.*

"But they that wait upon the LORD shall renew their strength; they shall mount up with wings as eagles; they shall run, and not be weary; and they shall walk, and not faint." Isaiah 40:31

The word *waiting,* in this passage, has nothing to do with sitting around and doing nothing. That's what we have interpreted it to say in our English vernacular. No, the Hebrew meaning is, to not lose your expectation. Do not allow what's happening around you to stop your expectation for something greater to come to you while you are seeking to grow, to be changed and to prosper.

Waiting, as in serving the Lord, doesn't mean to sit around in some mystic, trance like state, chanting some kind of prayer. It means, serve God in the midst of your crisis; expecting great things to come. Don't like your job... not making enough money? Stop praying about it and find another job, a better job. Try it! Seek, look, you will find. God has something better out there; you just have to pursue it.

Worship while you wait. Worship while you're still in hard times. Serve God and be faithful. I promise you, the blessing has already been sent. Expect it!

WHAT IS WORSHIP?

First of all, singing or music by itself is not worship. Music plays an important part, but it is only the vehicle by which we enter. Music powerfully communicates culture. Music is very important in describing what and who we are as a church body. A great and powerful sermon can be canceled out by lifeless music.

You could say our culture reflects our worship, but what kind of music is God concerned with. Does God like hymns more than charismatic music... would He rather us be contemporary, or country in our approach? I don't believe that style is the issue. God is only concerned with the attitude, or our hearts, not the form of our expressions.

TRADITIONS - ARE THEY GOOD OR BAD?

Traditions within themselves are great... but when it starts to cancel out the move and power of God, tradition becomes evil and wrong. The problem with tradition is that it fears change. Each tradition is suspicious of the other and often reinforces its own uniqueness to justify its existence. Change challenges that uniqueness.

TRUE WORSHIPPERS:

"But the hour cometh, and now is, when the true worshippers shall worship the Father in spirit and in truth: for the Father seeketh such to worship him. God is a Spirit: and they that worship him must worship him in spirit and in truth." John 4:23-24

Jesus informs us that a true worshipper would worship in **"SPIRIT AND IN TRUTH."** Not either or, but both. If we love to flow in the Spirit, but are impatient with the process of making careful observations, we are not yet the kind of worshipers God is looking for and rain is withheld. If we are diligent students, yet you cannot make room for someone to base a claim of revelation, we are not yet the worshipers that please God.

The New Testament declares to us the way in which we should be setting up our worship services.

"See then that ye walk circumspectly, not as fools, but as wise, redeeming the time, because the days are evil. wherefore be ye not unwise, but understanding what the will of the Lord is. And be not drunk with wine, wherein is excess; but be filled with the Spirit; Speaking to yourselves **in psalms** *and* **hymns** *and* **spiritual songs**, *singing and* **making melody in your heart** *to the Lord;* **Giving thanks** *always for all things unto God and the Father in the name of our Lord Jesus Christ;* **Submitting yourselves** *one to another in the fear of God". Ephesians 5:15-21*

"Some charismatic churches tend to sing choruses to the exclusion of hymns. Some traditional churches sing hymns to the exclusion of choruses. And a very small percentage of all churches have any significant experience with spiritual songs. Yet, God's Word invites us all to express our gratitude through all three song forms." Worship is unity within diversity.

The protocol of a worship service:
1. Be filled with the Spirit.
2. Speaking to ourselves in psalms, hymns, and spiritual songs.
3. Singing and making melody in your heart to the Lord.
4. Thanksgiving is the source of our singing.
5. Giving thanks for all things.
6. Submitting to one another in love.
7. Walk in the fear of God.

"The hills melted like wax at the presence of the LORD, at the presence of the Lord of the whole earth." Psalm 97:5

Face down on the floor I lay crying and pouring my soul out to the Lord. All around me I could hear the crying and the heart of the people who were also moved to tears by what had entered the room. My Praise and Worship Pastor, Raymond Hollis, along with the musicians were playing and singing to the Lord whatever came in their hearts. It was our prayer time, and the more we tarried in that place, the more I began to melt in the presence of God.

Several were stretched out all over; their arms extended. We were all overwhelmed by the revealed nearness of the true God. We all began to melt like wax... Wrong was exposed, and right was entering in. The rain of Heaven was falling down upon us. First, it was just a sprinkle, but soon, we began to experience an **outpouring;** as if the clouds overhead had erupted and we were becoming soaked by the rain. God was revealing Himself to us.

No worship no rain
Since the creation of man, God has revealed Himself to mankind. He has a desire to show Himself to His people. As our heavenly Father, He is relational. He wants to be near to those He has created. The Bible is full of people who have experienced this dimension of God's presence.

There are two passageways into God's revealed presence, or nearness.

One is prayer: Most people know that they can experience a communion with the Lord in prolonged prayer, but the word synonymous with His presence is Praise: *"Thou are holy, O thou that inhabit the praises of Israel." (Psalm 22:3)* Is it any wonder that there will be singing for all eternity?

Second is Praise: It is in praise and worship that we can encounter His presence revealed. We can literally sing our way into the presence of the Lord. I believe singing is the quickest way into His presence. Sing before we pray.

For those who say they do not sing well or can't carry a tune; let me inform you that God is not listening to our voice quality. He listens to our heart. We are to sing to the Lord in our daily worship.

FACTS ABOUT GOD:

- God is good. (Psalm 86:5)
- God is always ready to forgive. (Psalm 86:5)
- God is plenteous in mercy. (Psalm 86:5)
- God shows mercy to those who pursue Him for it. (Psalm 86:5)
- God answers those who call for Him when trouble comes. (Psalm 86:7)
- God is unlike every other power, or authority. (Psalm 86:8)
- God has enemies. (Psalm 83:1-2)

WORSHIP IS RECOGNITION:

Worship is recognizing that God is your real love and source. Worship is ascribing worth to something. "Worth-ship" is worship! When we lift up our hearts and sing with our mouths, we are ascribing worth to God, not that God needs us to identify Him. God does not suffer from an identity crisis; however, He deserves to be recognized as your King. I believe that people who have a hard time really worshipping God haven't found Jesus.

Have you ever noticed that the church is usually half full during the praise and worship time? Nearing the end, you'll see all kinds of people coming into the church to listen to the message. The same people who come in late seem to also be the ones to leave early. Now think for a moment, why should God rain anything upon those people? Praise and worship is for God, and preaching the Word is for man. When we come in late for praise and worship but make sure we are there for the preaching, we are, in a sense, saying that God's time isn't as important as our time. This could be the very reason God has shut up His Heavens over your life.

WHAT'S HAPPENING AROUND US IS DIRECTLY CONNECTED TO WHAT'S HAPPENING IN US.

Whatever we are focused on is what is mastering us at that time. I want to turn all my focus upon Jesus. He's the One I want to master me... mentor me... train me... promote me. What is your center? Whatever is at your center, you will attract. If money is your center, then money is all you will attract... If anger is your center, you will attract anger. It is important to make Jesus the center of all that you do. When Jesus is your center, you will attract everything you will ever need; money, a home, a family, joy, peace, happiness and so much more. Jesus said, *"Seek first the Kingdom, and all these things will be added unto to you."* What things? All things that are needed!

WHAT IS HAPPENING IN US COULD BE DECIDING WHAT IS HAPPENING AROUND US!

Proper worship builds in our minds the right focus. Worship is a key ingredient to build a proper mindset. Worship is not an option; worship is a necessity for favor and spiritual growth.

Thoughts create feelings, and feelings create actions. Worship is a thought that is acted out in our emotions. When we worship, we change the thought process from negative to positive.

FACTS ABOUT WORSHIP:
- Worship can stop the mind from wandering off the right path of peace and prosperity.
- Worship can produce victory and joy in moments.
- Worship can stop the enemy in his tracks and keep your mind free from fear and worry.
- Worship can open the prison of captivity and loosen the chains of hurt from you. (Acts 16)
- Worship can free those around you who are also in captivity. (Acts 16)
- Worship destroys the chains that have held you in bondage.
- Worship can build your sense of security and faith.
- Religion attempts to stop real worship.

Document Your Journey

TOPIC	THOUGHT

CHAPTER TEN

WHERE THE RIVER FLOWS, THE FISH LIVE

*"...because this water flows there and makes the salt water fresh; so where **the river flows everything will live**."*
Ezekial 47:6-10 NIV

WHERE THE RIVER FLOWS, THE FISH LIVE...

"Then he led me back to the bank of the river. When I arrived there, I saw a great number of trees on each side of the river. He said to me, "This water flows toward the eastern region and goes down into the Arabah, where it enters the Sea. When it empties into the Sea, the water there becomes fresh. Swarms of living creatures will live wherever the river flows. There will be large numbers of fish, because this water flows there and makes the salt water fresh; so where the river flows everything will live." Ezekiel 47:6-10 NIV

Where the river flows, the fish live. Rain that falls from heaven causes the rivers to flow and to grow. Without rain, the rivers would dry up and those directly connected to those rivers, would dry up also.

When we stop the rain, we stop life. What opens the heavens and causes us to experience rain?

First, is our giving; your tithe will cause the windows of heaven to swing wide open. God says that when those windows are open, He would pour out such a blessing that there would not be room enough to contain it.

MONEY MATTERS TO GOD

The Bible speaks over two thousand times about our giving of money. The Bible speaks more about prosperity and giving than it does about heaven and hell; yet, we are always preaching about everything but money and how to get it.

There's a false teaching that tithing isn't a New Testament

requirement. This is a farce. Those who teach this are completely out of order and disqualify for the position of pastor or bishop.

Let's just say for argument sake that you believe that. Well then, you must understand that giving is still a part of the New Testament. The word that Paul likes to use about our giving is the word liberal, or bountifully, or generously, depending on what translation you are reading.

I did a little test in my church. I handed out ten chips and said, "If this was a blessing from God, take a generous portion from it and give it back to me." Every person gave me back a percentage that was higher than the tenth. Some did twenty percent, others thirty and forty percent. Some even went as high as fifty to sixty percent.

It is apparent that generous is taken as an abundant amount. If the tithe bothers you and you are under the persuasion that tithe isn't a New Testament requirement you still have to give. Since giving is a part of the New Testament, then start giving a portion of your income. Remember, to be obedient you have to give generously.

IF YOU INSIST ON TAKING WHAT GOD DIDN'T GIVE YOU, HE'LL TAKE WHAT HE GAVE YOU AND LET YOU KEEP WHAT YOU TOOK.

He gave Adam the garden. God told Adam that the tree of knowledge of good and evil was His. The tree of life represented the tithe. Adam took the tree of life. God let him keep the tree of knowledge, but He took the garden.

He gave Ahab the nation. Ahab took Naboth's vineyard and killed him to get it. God said, "Keep the vineyard," but He took back the nation.

He gave you the ninety, but if you insist on taking the tithe, He'll take back the ninety. Giving opens the windows of Heaven. When those windows are open you can expect the rain to fall. Remember, rain produces and supplies the river and where the river flows, the fish live!

Second, is our prayer life; when we pray, God

responds. Prayer enters the heart of God and God responds to those prayers. Paul said that he had confidence that when he prayed God heard him.

Third, is our praise; praise causes God to leave where He is and enter where praise is being offered up. *"But thou art holy, O thou that inhabitest the praises of Israel" (Psalm 22:3).* God loves praise! Usually the first thing that goes in our growing church is the singing. We begin to make cuts to shrink up the time so that we can attract more people. Maybe our focus shouldn't be more people, but more of God. The quickest and easiest way into His presence is singing. Increase the praise and you will increase His presence.

THE RIVER PRODUCES LIFE:

The proof that the river is flowing is that dead things live. When the river of life is flowing through your church, people begin to change. To live is to change. If you're not changing, you're not in the right river. **The proof of His presence is change!** Get out of your church if you are not changing! The river that flows creates life, life produces growth and growth produces change. If we're not careful, we will try to validate our religion, and in the process, void out our relationship with God. When we discover the need to defend our denomination more than dominating in our dominion, we have left the river of life and entered the river of religion.

There are **two rivers.** In Revelation *chapter twelve,* we read about the dragon that shows up and spews water out of its mouth. Now, we all know that dragons spew fire, not water. If the enemy shows up with his fire, we will recognize him and cast him out. So the enemy has changed tactics. He comes as an angel of light. He shows up as being a lover of God. He's learned how to look like us and walk like us. He has made a counterfeit river called religion. *(2 Corinthians. 11:14)*

- Religion hates better than it loves.
- Religion condemns better than it comforts.

- Religion accuses rather than covers.
- Religion conforms better than it transforms.
- Religion is offended rather than convicted.
- Religion confuses better than it constructs.
- Religion deceives people rather than deliver them.
- Religion argues better than it agrees.

Religion has all the flavor and force of the river, yet it is missing one main factor. That factor is that everywhere the river flows, **the fish live**. Not true for the false counterfeit river, for where it flows, the fish die.

The river of life leads you to the ocean of prosperity and peace. The river of religion leads you to the swamplands of stench and death.

Diversity is the proof that there is life in the river. (Ezk. 47:9) There shall be a great multitude of fish in this river. The proof of the river of life is that all kinds will find acceptance in it. There will be no separation of race or color. The river will change what we see, and what we will see is that we all live and belong in the river. Once you passed the blood line of Jesus, you should have dealt with the race line of color. Jesus sees no color. Let me inform you. Poverty, sickness, disease, depression and the like have no racial preference. NEITHER SHOULD WE!

THE RIVER ABIDES WITHIN.

"He that believeth on me, as the scripture hath said, out of his belly shall flow rivers of living water" (John 7:38). The river survives in us. How does it flow from us to others? Through our words! Life and death are in the power of the tongue. The river flows through our speaking. What we say determines what we are to receive. Your mouth lays claim to your future. The river flows through us to those who are hurting and need healing. The river flows and the fish live! This is why it is necessary for the rain of heaven to fall upon us. The rain causes a river to overflow. When we are under the outpouring of the rain of the Spirit, it forces the river in us to swell and overflow its boundaries. When the river exceeds its boundaries, it causes more of God to be

manifested in and through you. We can either open our mouths and let the river flow, or shut our mouths and dam up the flow of blessing and healing in our lives, church and families.

THE RIVER FORCES WHAT IS NOT GODLY TO EXIT YOUR LIFE.

Have you ever seen what a river can do when it is at flood stage? When the rains keep falling and force the river to swell? The largest of obstacles can be removed in a matter of minutes. I believe the same it true with us. When the river is flowing around us and through us, it forces what doesn't belong to exit our lives. In a matter of moments, what has been holding us down and causing our failure can be uprooted and removed from our lives. Go ahead, release the river of life! Not everyone in your life belongs in your life. What you have allowed to stay around you could be costing you the river. When the river is flowing through you, it will force what's not of it out of you. Do you know what I say? LET THE RIVER FLOW!

THE RIVER REVEALS TO US WHAT WE NEED TO KNOW TO INCREASE FOR THE KINGDOM OF GOD.

There are two orders in the church.

First, there's the order of "Priest." This is the ability to minister to the Lord. Then, there is the "Apostolic" order; the ability to prophesy. Everyone wants the power to speak to crisis and situations. There's this high surge of desire for power, yet the power only comes through first walking in your priestly calling. We are all called to walk as priests of the Most High God. Our ability to minister to the Lord will build in us our ability to minister to others. The river produces the life sustaining power to walk in these two orders. Of course, you know that the river is Jesus.

Revelation without wisdom can be divisive. Revelation without the wisdom of understanding it will cause us to judge others instead of causing us to grow deeper. Churches, ministries and businesses have been destroyed because revelation without wisdom can be disruptive.

THE PROOF THAT GOD'S RIVER IS FLOWING IS DIVERSITY:

Swarms of living creatures will live wherever the river flows. There will be large numbers of fish, because this water flows there and makes the salt water fresh; (Ezekial47:9-10)

There isn't just one race or one way of doing things. The river produces diversity. Diversity is good. It's healthy for a church or ministry to reach everyone in their city. There are diverse gifts and diverse ministries but one Lord, one Spirit and one God.

I have a problem when we see only one kind of people sitting in our local assemblies. That makes me want to question why? Why does everyone seem to be a cookie cut image of what's around them? The river produces diversity. Now, diversity doesn't mean there is no unity. Unity is the ability to walk in different personalities and different assignments, but all having a common goal. When each is walking or working in their lane, the river flourishes and grows.

I'm not just speaking about color. I'm also talking about ideas, personalities and economic status. When we are in the river of God, we are able to get along while we are going along.

THE RIVER PRODUCES INNER PEACE

Peace that we have heard about for years. Peace that passes all understanding. This peace is an internal peace. The river brings the power of a secure identity. Let me tell you the truth. There is no real peace like internal peace... knowing who you are! When we fix the internal identity battle, there will be no more room for allowing others to determine your self worth.

The cross is easier to carry when you know your identity beneath it. Jesus could carry His cross because He had a sure foundation of who He was. Also, Jesus had great faith in the Holy Spirit. He trusted Him enough to surrender to death, knowing that the Holy Spirit would raise Him in three days. Now that's internal peace!

The proof of a secure identity is discerning and embracing your difference.

Your difference is what makes you important. If you don't know your difference, you can't grow your difference. Your difference is what will give you your identity. Once you have discovered your difference celebrate it, market and sell it. Build your life around your difference!

THE CROSS IS NOT SO HEAVY WHEN YOU KNOW YOUR IDENTITY BENEATH IT.

- **Difference decides who belongs in your life.**
- **Difference decides who doesn't belong in your life.**
- **The dominant difference between people is who they have chosen to believe.**

When you know your difference, jealousy ceases... envy ceases... anger and bitterness can be dealt with. Worry and fear ceases.

Knowing your difference can make you so authoritative in your present, that your future will enter your life and beg you to get in it.

The difference in people is what they see. David saw opportunity while others saw opposition. Joseph knew his difference. That's the reason he succeeded when all hell broke out in his life. The rains from Heaven can promote your difference.

Difference decides access. Who sees you determines your promotion. People decide your season. Favor is simply when someone is willing to leave their season and enter yours to help you get in theirs. Imagine Ruth without a Naomi, Elisha without an Elijah. One single sentence from the right person can change your life forever... you can move from the prison to the palace.

WAYS TO LOSE ACCESS

1. Listening to wrong voices.
2. Disrespecting those you have access to
3. Disagreement that causes you to become angry
4. Dissension that grows evil thinking.
5. Disloyalty and Disappointments

The greatest access in your life is God. *"Let us therefore come boldly to the throne of grace that we may obtain mercy and find grace to help in time of need" (Hebrews 4:16 NKJV).* Access trivialized is access lost. Many have, for too long, trivialized the access that God has given them and now they have lost it. I pray right now that the heavens will open and the rain will fall over your life.

THE HOLY SPIRIT IS THE FORCE BEHIND THE RIVER

What Peter couldn't do walking with Jesus for three years; he did in a day when the Holy Spirit entered him. Think for a moment how necessary the infilling of the Holy Spirit is. What could we accomplish if we had the gift of the Holy Spirit working in us? I mean all the gifts, not just what our denominations say we can have or should have.

The gift of (speaking in) tongues is a powerful gift. What the mind can not put into words, the Holy Spirit can give us in tongues. Many of us have misunderstood the power of speaking in tongues.

Some have been under the persuasion that tongues were only a gift given to the Apostles and when the apostolic authority left, so did the power and the gift. However, if you carefully study the book of Acts, you are going to find out that the gift of tongues wasn't just given to the Apostles. In Acts chapter two, the first encounter we have; we find out that there were more in the upper room than just the Apostles.

"And suddenly there came a sound from heaven as of a rushing mighty wind, and it filled all the (the entire)

house where they were sitting. And there appeared unto them cloven tongues like as of fire, and it sat upon each of them. And they were all filled with the Holy Ghost, and began to speak with other tongues, as the Spirit gave them utterance." Acts 2: 3- 4

Notice that all were filled. This means that those who weren't Apostles were given the gift, or better, a prayer language in tongues. Still need more?

In Acts chapter ten, there was a man named Cornelius, who was an Italian musician (vs.1). Cornelius obviously had a personal encounter with the Hebrew God, but because he was not a Hebrew he was not allowed in the church. So every week he would send his money, his giving, his tithe and offering. Want to talk about racism; here it is at its best. You're not allowed in, but we'll take your money. What happens next is what amazes me.

God takes notice of Cornelius's lifestyle and sacrifice. *"...Thy prayers and thine alms are come up for a memorial before God..." (Acts 10:4).* Notice that his giving came up to God as a memorial. Memorial means monument. His giving was a picture in the mind of God. A memory God could not erase. Our last seed, offering or gift is God's last memory of us. WOW!

Let me get back to the point. Cornelius wasn't an Apostle. He wasn't even a Hebrew. God wanted to give Cornelius something, so He sent Peter to him, not just to pray for him or to allow him to come to church, but for much more. (Read all the scriptures below.)

"And the following day they entered Caesarea. Now Cornelius was waiting for them, and had called together his relatives and close friends. As Peter was coming in, Cornelius met him and fell down at his feet and worshiped him. but Peter lifted him up, saying, "Stand up; I myself am also a man." Acts 10:24-26 NKJV

"Cornelius, your prayer has been heard, and your alms

are remembered in the sight of God. Send therefore to Joppa and call Simon here, whose surname is Peter. He is lodging in the house of Simon, a tanner, by the sea. When he comes, he will speak to you.' "So I sent to you immediately, and you have done well to come. Now therefore, we are all present before God, to hear all the things commanded you by God. "Then Peter opened his mouth and said: "In truth I perceive that God shows no partiality.   But in every nation whoever fears Him and works righteousness is accepted by Him."
Acts 10:31-35 NKJV

*"While Peter was still speaking these words, the Holy Spirit fell upon all those who heard the word. And those of the circumcision who believed were astonished**, as many as came with Peter, because the gift of the Holy Spirit had been poured out on the Gentiles also. For they heard them speak with tongues and magnify God.** Then Peter answered, can anyone forbid water, that these should not be baptized who have received the Holy Spirit just as we have?" And he commanded them to be baptized in the name of the Lord. Then they asked him to stay a few days." Acts 10:44-48 NKJV*

What did Cornelius and the other Gentiles get? What were they filled with? What was the proof of that filling? Yes, they **spoke in tongues**. Now this is years later. Not just days. Years later, God saw fit to pour into the Gentiles and Cornelius the gift of speaking in tongues. Now, if you don't believe in the gift, I challenge you to find in the Bible where it says that God has taken that gift away?

If you don't want this gift that's one thing, but stop denying that it is real and that it is still available today. Stop lying to yourself. If you fear it, or don't believe in it, you could be denying yourself the greatest spiritual blessing. A language that dumbfounds the enemy and only God can understand.

It's obvious that God wants to speak and that He can speak in different languages. Every country has its own language. We know that biblically, Heaven is a different place and has citizenship. If Heaven is a different place with different rules and has a citizenship, why can't we believe that there would be a heavenly language. (Philippians 3:20)

Master the secret power of continuous conversation with the Holy Spirit.

Give your spiritual language a focus. Praying in tongues is not just something we do to fill up our prayer life when we run out of what to say. Tongues are a language. Tongues are a conversation in the ears of God. Command your mind to focus and then pray in the Holy Ghost. What your mind can not phrase – the Holy Spirit will. Tongues can and will build your faith. I don't want anything my faith cannot produce. I don't want anything God did not give me.

Document Your Journey

TOPIC	THOUGHT

CHAPTER ELEVEN

KNOW WHERE "THERE" IS

"I also withheld rain from you, when there were still three months to the harvest. I made it rain on one city; **I withheld rain from another city.** *One part was rained upon, And where it did not rain the part withered."*
Amos 4:7 NKJV

GEOGRAPHY MATTERS

*W*here you are is just as important as what you are doing. If you are the right person in the wrong place, it will not rain. If you are the wrong person in the right place, it still will not rain. You have to be the right person, in the right place, if you desire to see an abundance of rain.

There were places before there were people. Places matter! You can travel all over the world, but if you do not discern where *there* is, you will never discover your blessing.

YOU MUST DISCERN WHERE "THERE" IS!

*"Then the word of the LORD came to him, saying, "Get away from here and turn eastward, and hide by the Brook Cherith, which flows into the Jordan. And it will be that you shall drink from the brook, and I have commanded the ravens to feed you **there**." 1 Kings 17:2-5 NKJV*

"PROSPERITY IS SCHEDULED TO THE RIGHT PLACE"

Elijah could go anywhere he wanted, but if he ignored the place where God instructed, he would have died in the drought. *"There"* is a powerful revelation. *"There"* is where the raven is scheduled to feed you and the water is ready to quench your thirst. So many have missed their opportunity for abundance and substance simply because they refuse to discern and obey where *"there"* is. How about you? Have you missed your abundance because you are in the wrong place trying to make something happen? Are you in a dead church knowing you haven't been fed in years, but stay because you have been believing a lie that your suppose to be there? Could you be missing out on what God has intended in your life?

SEASONS CHANGE:
Seasons change and when they do, expect a change of pace, a change of place and a change of race:

> "...and it happened after a while that the brook dried up, because there had been no rain in the land." 1 Kings 17:7 NKJV

Notice the brook dried up, the raven stop bringing the food source and the blessings and the water to drink all ceased. What did the prophet do? Did he start confessing and working his faith to restart the flow of blessings? No, he did not. That's what some of us would have done because we were taught drought and famine couldn't be the will of God. However, it was God who dried up the brook; it was God who stopped sending the food source. It would have been useless, and in my opinion very costly if the prophet would have started confessing and believing for provision. No matter how he worked his faith, if God is the source behind the crisis, your faith isn't going to work. Faith must be attached to God's plan and purpose. God was done with Elijah in Cherith. God was ready to change his season; to move him into a greater place with an even greater assignment. That assignment was now placed on him. He was going to be the raven for someone else. The dimension of blessing changed.

> "Then the word of the Lord came to him, saying, "Arise, go to Zarephath, which belongs to Sidon, and dwell there. See, I have commanded a widow there to provide for you." So he arose and went to Zarephath. And when he came to the gate of the city, indeed a widow was there gathering   sticks. And he called to her and said, "Please

bring me a little water in a cup that I may drink." And as she was going to get it, he called to he and said, "Please bring me a morsel of bread in your hand." 1 Kings 17:8-11 NKJV

You must know where **"there"** is! To have this understanding would ease a great burden in your future. When things seem to go wrong, or the river of substance dries up, it may not be anything but God changing your season.

God was now sending His man to Zarephath. He was adding to the equation a widow and her son. God told the prophet that He, God, would command the widow there to provide for him, but when Elijah arrived, he found the widow picking up sticks. She informed the prophet that she was going to cook her and her son a cake, live for today but tomorrow they would starve and die like everyone else in the famine.

Here is where the story gets tricky to me. God said that He would command the widow to provide for Him; however, when the prophet arrived, she acted like she didn't know him. She let him know right away that she intended to feed herself and her son. No where in the passage do we see God talking to her... much less commanding her to take care of Elijah. This seems to be a contradiction, but could there be something deeper that causes a release of even something greater? **Let's see!**

The prophet asked for water to drink. It hadn't rained in sometime but the widow didn't hesitate to supply him with water. However, when Elijah asked for a cake, some food, she seemed to have a problem with that request.

"So she said, "As the Lord your God lives, I do not have bread, only a handful of flour in a bin, and a little oil in a jar; and see, I am gathering a couple of sticks that I may go in and prepare it for myself and my son, that we may eat it, and die." 1 Kings 17:12 NKJV

Her response would be my response. "Sir, as the Lord

your God lives, I do not have enough bread and oil to feed you and my family." Her mind was not focused on her future; her mind was connected to her present.

I thought God commanded her! God said he commanded her to provide, but here in this passage the widow acted like the request was the craziest thing she had ever heard.

The first time, Elijah asked her as a request. The second time he changes his tactics and gave her an instruction.

"And Elijah said to her, "Do not fear; go and do as you have said, but make me a small cake from it first, and bring it to me; and afterward make some for yourself and your son. For thus says the Lord God of Israel: 'The bin of flour shall not be used up, nor shall the jar of oil run dry, until the day the Lord sends rain on the earth." 1 Kings 17:13-14 NKJV

Do not fear. Fear was the first thing that stopped her from obeying the man of God's voice. Fear is the opposite of what faith can do. Fear will cause your mind to negotiate and try to figure out how. How can this be... how can what I have become more? The spirit of fear will create a paralyzed believer.

Go, and do as you have said, except do the Lord's work first. **Make mine first. <u>Sequence matters to God.</u>** The law of giving is to always take a portion of what you have and break off a piece for the work of the Lord. This will always release God's rain over your life. Notice that the prophet doesn't try to convince her that he's a man of God. Elijah doesn't show her the picture of his needs and how his ministry is suffering. He doesn't speak about the dead raven and dried up brooks in his life. What He does do is start talking to her faith. He begins to build her a picture of her future, her harvest, and puts her doubts in the rear of her mind.

> **PAINT A PICTURE OF YOUR HARVEST THAT IS CLEARER THAN THE PICTURE OF YOUR LACK.**

Paint a picture of your harvest that is clearer than the picture of your lack... Look at the prophet's reaction to her. Thus says the Lord, Your meal barrel will not be used up nor will your oil jar run dry, until the day the Lord sends rain on the earth. Her willingness to see past her need and into her seed decided her longevity. She decided to obey even though the instruction seemed irrational. God will sometimes give us irrational instructions but know for sure they will never be impossible with Him.

> *"So she went away and did according to the word of Elijah; and she and he and her household ate for many days. The bin of flour was not used up, nor did the jar of oil run dry, according to the word of the Lord which He spoke by Elijah". 1 Kings 17:15-17 NKJV*

She obeyed. She did what seemed impossible and irrational. God didn't just take care of Elijah, nor did He just take care of the widow and the son. Look at the verses closer. *"She, and he and her household ate, survived, and flourished for many days."* It wasn't just her son, or just the prophet, or just her who ate, but anyone connected to her in her household was experiencing the overflow of her harvest. The rain of Heaven was falling before the rain came that ended the drought. WOW! I want to experience this kind of power. Do you? For this to take place in our lives we are going to have to experience droughts. We are going to have to be in a bad place. Living in a crisis this is where the greatest rain of God can fall. It's in those moments where you believe you only have enough for today. In that moment, here comes the Man of God, here comes God. He will send us a deliverer and if we can recognize God in the man as the widow did, we too can walk out many days experiencing a miracle when we should have experienced defeat and death. It is all predicated on our decision to believe. It will be our decision to sow, to release what we have to God so He can make it more than it is. Decisions decide God's release. What if she would have refused? She would have died broke and hungry. This wouldn't have been God's fault, nor would it have been Elijah's fault. It would have been her wrong decision.

Wrong decisions trigger the law of unintended consequences. Have you made wrong decisions that have kept you in the land of bondage? It's possible to be freed from the hand of bondage, and still be bound up in the land of bondage.

> *"So I have come down to deliver them **out of the hand of the Egyptians**, and to **bring them up from that land to a good and large land**, to a land flowing with milk and honey, to the place of the Canaanites and the Hittites and the Amorites and the Perizzites and the Hivites and the Jebusites." Exodus 3:8-9 NKJV*

COMFORT CREATES CONFORMITY! God was going to deliver them out of the hand of bondage. The hand of bondage is the bondage that keeps us from moving. The hand of bondage stops momentum. It stops our movement to other places; however, if God only delivers us from the hand of bondage, we can still be in captivity in the land of bondage. The children of Israel didn't start out in bondage, **but they stayed in the wrong place too long.** God never intended for them to live in Egypt as long as they did. The children of Israel became comfortable with the handout of their enemy. Abnormal became normal. God knew that delivering them from the hand of bondage would only give them a false sense of freedom. They had to become free enough to become frustrated.

Comfort is one of the easiest ways to fall into a lifestyle of believing only what others tell you, and not what is really the truth. We accept our lives and believe that God wants us to be happy in a lifestyle of pain. Religion calls this content, or satisfied. Religion says that if we are broke, then it must be God's will. Come on! You know deep down inside that this is not the case. God wants all of His children to be blessed. Now, am I saying that we all must be at the same level... financially, mentally, spiritually? No! Life is made up of levels. If we were all at the same level, there would be no need for teachers, mentors or instructors. I am saying that God wants us to be better than we are; to grow stronger, bigger and more equipped to handle life. Comfort stops change. Comfort creates conformity and conformity stops change.

So He says, *"I will bring them up from the land to a good and large land..."* **The land represents their mentality**. If God had not brought them out of the land of bondage; even though they were free from the hand, they would still have been bound to the mindset of slavery. Now, mental bondage is more crippling than physical bondage. I can shackle your hands and feet, but if your mind is free, you are really free. It doesn't matter what kind of physical prison you're in, your mind is where you maintain your identity and valor. Your mind decides your freedom not your circumstances.

Your mind is your world. The world you live in is not the world you really live in. The world you think you live in is your reality. ***"As a man thinks so is he...." (Proverbs 23:7)***

Their geography, where they were, was as important to their freedom as to who they were. To free yourself totally from the hand of the enemy, you're going to have to move from the land of the enemy. God wanted to bring them from a lifestyle of portions into a lifestyle of abundance. (John 10:10) It was a larger land. It was a land flowing with milk and honey. Their

CONFORMITY STOPS CHANGE

present state of living was at the mercy of the enemy. As long as they were doing what was expected, they were fed a portion. In this place, there was never enough.

The *land of portions* is the place where you only eat what someone else says you can eat. You can only possess what someone else gives you. It is the land of welfare. Isn't it strange that God didn't immediately give them their abundance when He brought them out of the land,. but He took His people on a journey through the wilderness and kept them living on portions? So, what changed? A lot! They were now being sustained by God's hand, not the enemy. They were being processed to their promise. God was giving them portions to get them to another land. He was not just giving them less, He was taking them to *just enough.* Before, they weren't getting enough, but in the wilderness, they got just enough. They were being processed to their promise.

The first lesson of moving from one place to another is to learn that God wants to bless you first, from His own hand. He desires your increase to come, not by your works only, nor by your education only not even by your abilities, but by the Lord's hand.

God was blessing them and they didn't have to do anything but follow Him. He established a connection with His people before releasing them to the rains of abundance.

The children of Israel had a problem with being thankful... they complained all the time. They had lost sight of the fact that they used to be in bondage, but were now being fed and loved by God.

Being unthankful is a sign that you may have a thinking problem.

God gave them portions to gain their trust. He was establishing them as His people and wanted them to know that no matter what, He was their God. The children of Israel couldn't see beyond what was left at their tent each day. They wouldn't stop long enough to see that their clothes never wore out, nor did their shoes ever have to be replaced. They failed to recognize that when it rained in the camp, it rained food; bread, sweet bread. They were in bondage to the land! They were so caught up in where they were that they failed to realize where they were going. They were being led to a land that was larger and bigger than the land of Egypt. They were not going to be at the mercy of anyone else in their lives. They were making a transition from being the conquered, to being more than a conqueror. They were about to experience a life where there would be NO MORE PORTIONS!

NO MORE PORTIONS:

The abundant life was their destiny; just like it is for you and me. God sent His Son Jesus, so that you and I could be free, not just from the hand of bondage but also the land.

> *"The thief does not come except to steal, and to kill, and to destroy. I have come that they may have life, and that they may have it more abundantly." John 10:10 NKJV*

The thief is the hand in the land of bondage. Jesus said that He came for a purpose. His purpose wasn't just to open Heaven and give us an eternal home. His purpose was to establish the Kingdom. His purpose was to give us life. Right *now* life! Not just a life of existence, but a life of abundance! Jesus died to create a larger land for you to live in, a land flowing with milk and honey; a blessed land.

Are you eating the abundant grapes of love and prosperity, or are you eating the sour grapes of just surviving? The time for survival is over! It's time to start living! NO MORE PORTIONS!

Have you noticed how it seems to rain blessings on some people and not on others? You can be sitting in the same church with someone and they always seem to be getting the blessings. Haven't you ever asked why? Think for a moment! They're sitting in the same place, hearing the same preaching, singing the same songs yet they're increasing and your not.

They have mastered the law of geography. They may be sitting where you are, but they're not mentally where you are. The hand may have been lifted off of your life, but you're still in bondage to the land (geography). Make up your mind right now to experience all of God's blessings.

Stop allowing what others are saying to keep you from your destiny.

You have been destined for the best. Believe that! Accept it! Expect good things to happen to you every day. Wake up with an expectation that the favor of God is going to happen to you today. (Psalm 68:19) The Bible says that God loads us down daily with benefits. The rain that falls from Heaven is the rain that brings abundance... healing... peace... security... healing... wealth... wholeness... understanding. This rain is the rain of glory. The latter day and former day rain mingled together.

The natural rain falls and waters what needs to be watered for growth and cleanses what needs to be cleansed. As it falls, it also removes particles that pollute the atmosphere. Have you ever stopped and noticed the air after a good hard rain? The air is clean and crystal clear. The same is true when spiritual rain falls from God's presence. When you're in a struggle and don't know what to do, pray for rain! When you're under attack, pray for the rain from heaven to fall... seek the rain! Remember, rain is a sign that Heaven is open.

Lift up your eyes... do you see the clouds forming? The rain you've been seeking and fasting for is about to happen. Hurry! Get your umbrella! I just heard the sound of the abundance of rain!

Document Your Journey

TOPIC	THOUGHT

CHAPTER TWELVE

THE FORMER AND THE LATTER RAIN COMING DOWN TOGETHER

RAIN ON ME!

*"Be glad then, ye children of Zion, and rejoice in the LORD your God: for he hath **given you the former rain moderately, and he will cause to come down for you the rain, the former rain, and the latter rain in the first month.**" Joel 2:23*

*W*ow! This will be the day. Imagine what the church... no, imagine what those who are Kingdom Connected are going to experience when this last big serge of power and glory falls down upon us.

Notice the attitude that God wants us to have in these last days. The word says **Rejoice** and **be glad**. This won't be a time for us to live in worry. In the midst of all the sorrow... in the midst of all the pain... in the midst of all the poverty that will be around us on the earth, God says to rejoice and be glad. What's happening around us shouldn't be affecting what is happening in us.

THERE ARE NO BAD DAYS ONLY BAD MOMENTS

Let's look at all the words that mean rejoice; celebrate, expressed joy, to be pleased, cheerful, delighted and to be glad. Now, let's look at all the words that mean glad; happy, pleased, joyful, thankful and relieved. This is the attitude that God expects from us. Why? We are those who are going to live in the midst of the former and latter day outpouring. We are His remnant; the ones who have remained and who have endured. We are the true conquers; yet, what kind of Christians do you really see when you look around?

Denominational Christians; those who live and act the way they've been conditioned to act by their denominations.

As a whole, have we the called, the chosen, been the examples that we were destined to be? I think not - with our mega leaders divorcing... getting arrested over money issues...being charged with sexual misconduct. No wonder the world has questions about the God we speak of; not to mention how we act with each other; bitter, angry, offended and wounded all the time. We are ungrateful and mad about life. If you had to follow you, would you?

God wanted us to rejoice and be glad. Why? First of all, we are going to experience an outpouring of His presence that none has ever seen or read about. This spiritual, supernatural outpouring is mixed with who God was and what He is doing. Former and latter day rain! *"And the floors shall be full of wheat, and the fats shall overflow with wine and oil."(Joel 2 24)*

Secondly, we are going to experience restoration like never before. God is going to make the enemy put back every thing he has stolen or destroyed. *"And I will restore to you the years that the locust hath eaten, the cankerworm, and the caterpillar, and the palmerworm, my great army which I sent among you." (Joel 2:25)*

Thirdly, we are going to walk in a harvest of abundance that will make the enemy's head swim with anger and jealousy. God says we are going to walk and eat in plenty. Plenty means we will experience abundance, bountifully; there will be ample supply for everybody. It also means; here it comes, the word that a lot of people seem to get so angry about, prosperity. *"And ye shall eat in plenty, and be satisfied, and praise the name of the LORD your God that hath dealt wondrously with you: and my people shall never be ashamed."(Joel 2:26)*

Did you see that? You will eat in plenty, and in your life you will be satisfied. The life of prosperity produces that attitude of praise. Living in a place where you have lost your worries over your financial burden can be bliss. Think for a moment what it would be like if you were able to solve your financial problems?

That thought alone makes you want to praise the Name of the Lord. I hope you're not picking up that you can't praise in troubled times, but praise is sweeter when all of life becomes stress free. Stress free doesn't mean crisis free. Crisis will always be a part of life. There's no escaping that one law; however, living in these last days experiencing this latter and former day rain will set us up for some awesome praise.

Our praise is not just because we have enough supply. Our praise is based on how the Lord dealt with us. He didn't shut us out in our life of failure and sin. He didn't write us off when others gave up on us. Oh no! **He dealt with us wondrously.**

This praise isn't because we have enough... It won't be focused on the car, the house and the clothes. It won't be a focus on our materialistic world. Oh no, this praise is going to be lifted in the heights of the clouds where the rain is falling from. As we lift up our eyes and feel the rain from Heaven washing down our faces and down our bodies, we will be caught up in Him. As we are standing, hands lifted high, faces being wet with this latter day and former day rain, our voices will echo. Our voices will shout the thanksgiving and gratitude that we were not a people who were left to be accused by the enemy. We will experience the washing of our guilt... our shame... our condemnation. God has dealt wondrously with us. Can't you feel the rain already? Stop, can you hear that? It's the sound of thunder. God is about to open the heavens.

THE ACCUSER IS ALWAYS THE LOSER!

Never allow the enemy to shame you again. I don't care how bad you were or are. When you experience a life changing decision to make Jesus Christ your Lord and Savior those things are eradicated, eliminated, destroyed, laid to waste and useless. The accuser is always the loser. Satan is the loser!

Live your life in Isaiah 61:7, *"God took your shame and gave you double honor."* You're not to walk in shame; you're to walk in honor. So the next time someone lays the shame or blame on you, say *"Oh no, not shame on me... shame on Him."*

Jesus took my shame and traded it for His honor over my life.

If you've been saved for any length of time you probably have read the rest of that verse, so go ahead and take time to finish these verses.

"And ye shall know that I am in the midst of Israel, and that I am the LORD your God, and none else: and my people shall never be ashamed. And it shall come to pass afterward, that I will pour out my spirit upon all flesh; and your sons and your daughters shall prophesy, your old men shall dream dreams, your young men shall see visions: And also upon the servants and upon the handmaids in those days will I pour out my spirit. And I will shew wonders in the heavens and in the earth, blood, and fire, and pillars of smoke. The sun shall be turned into darkness, and the moon into blood, before the great and the terrible day of the LORD come." And it shall come to pass, that whosoever shall call on the name of the LORD shall be delivered: for in mount Zion and in Jerusalem shall be deliverance, as the LORD hath said, and in the remnant whom the LORD shall call." Joel 2:23-32

God is going to pour out His spirit on all of us! What a time to be alive. Stop crying about the times. Stop complaining about the gas prices, food prices and the economy. Position yourself for this latter day outpouring.

Pray for rain. Pray that the windows of Heaven will open over your life. Pray that it will rain over your finances, over your marriages, your children, your family and most of all over your entire church.

OPEN WINDOWS PRODUCE MAJOR BLESSINGS:

Paul "Bear" Bryant said, *"There is a big difference between wanting to and willing to..."*

Many in our churches want to be blessed. I can't imagine

anyone who would refuse the hand from another to increase and do better. The proof of that is to evaluate how much money all these states are making when they began to offer up a lottery. If the lottery earnings for a winner are always in the millions, think how much the profits to those winnings are.

For a moment let your thoughts drift. People are trying to win these millions by working one of God's major laws of increase. You go into a store and sow a seed in dollar increments with the expectation of winning millions. If you have ever purchased one of those lottery tickets you probably did what so many do. You sat down and discussed with excitement how you would spend the money. You would talk about who you would bless... what you would pay off... how much you would save... the house you would buy... the car you would drive. All that excitement and all you have is a ticket worth nothing... a ticket that you traded a dollar for, but if those numbers line up that one dollar ticket has now become your harvest.

Now, let me ask you a question. Why is it that people can flood to those stores and work the law of sowing and reaping and no one seems to be bothered by it? However, many of those same people leave church mad and upset when a man of God tells them that they can give their money into the Kingdom of God and expect God to send them a return; good measure, pressed down and shaken together(*Luke 6:38*).

They were just given the opportunity in that moment sow with a guarantee that those tickets, called offering envelopes, would pay off, and the minimum pay off from God is thirty-fold. (Mark 4:8) Let me give you a law that you cannot stop no matter how mad you get - Good seed falling on good soil always produces a harvest...no matter what.

GET SERIOUS ABOUT THE LAWS OF INCREASE:

God hasn't changed His laws of increase. Do you want a harvest? Wanting one is not enough. Are you willing to do what it takes to have the Lord open the windows of His good bounty and pour you out such a blessing there will not be room enough to receive it all? God has not changed. *"For I am the Lord, I do not change..." Malachi 3:6*

When you honor God, he's going to honor you. Are you willing to do what it takes to open God's financial window? We've talked about all kinds of rain and heavenly showers, but are you willing to do what it takes to receive and walk in financial blessings?

> *"Yet from the days of your fathers You have gone away from My ordinances And have not kept them. Return to Me, and I will return to you," Says the Lord of hosts. "But you said, 'In what way shall we return?" Malachi 3:7*

The book of Malachi is the last Old Testament book. It is going to be the last time God sends a prophetic word to his people. After this book, God shuts His mouth and doesn't speak for over four hundred years. Wouldn't you think that Malachi is what God wanted us to be thinking about until He opens His mouth in the book of Matthew?

IF YOU INSIST ON TAKING WHAT GOD DIDN'T GIVE YOU; HE'LL TAKE WHAT HE GAVE YOU AND LET YOU KEEP WHAT YOU TOOK.

God said from the days of your fathers you have gone away from my ordinances and have not kept them. Return to me, or better, return to those ordinances. When we return to God's laws we are actually returning to Him. Here's where people are always trying to escape the LAW. They say, where should we return... what should we return to? They act like they don't already know. God answers them.

STOP ROBBING GOD!

> *"Will a man rob God? Yet you have robbed Me! But you say, 'In what way have we robbed You?' In tithes and offerings." Malachi 3:8*

This interests me. How can someone rob God of money if He doesn't really need money? If you can't see God and you can't physically touch God, then why is He calling it robbery? In actuality, God gave you everything. If you hold back anything He has asked for, God considers it stealing.

They were robbing; stealing in their unwillingness to give their tithe, which is a tenth of all you've increased with. They al o robbed in their offerings, which I call seed.

If you insist on taking what God didn't give you, He'll take what He gave you and let you keep what you took. I've heard this said so many times by Dr. Murdock. Of course, he says it differently, but the meaning is the same. Could it be that the reason you're living in financial drought is that you've allowed someone to teach you incorrectly about the laws of increase? Giving really opens God's hand. Just maybe, God wants it to rain more than water... maybe it could rain money and all kinds of good stuff. Just a thought!

God gave King David a Kingdom and fame; David took Bathsheba. God let David keep Bathsheba, and God took his fame. *(2 Samuel 11)*

God gave Ahab the Nation; Ahab took Naboth's vineyard. God took back the nation and let him keep the vineyard. *(1 Kings 21)*

God gave Adam the garden; Adam took the tree of knowledge. God took back the garden and let him have the tree of knowledge (Genesis 3). **If you insist on taking what God didn't give you; He'll let you keep what you took; but He'll take back what He gave you.**

HE GAVE YOU THE NINETY; BUT IF YOU KEEP THE TITHE; HE'LL TAKE BACK THE NINETY AND LET YOU KEEP THE TITHE (10TH).

We are crazy fools. We are sometimes so blind to truth. How can we say we love God? How can we say we trust Him when we rob from God weekly by withholding what He has instructed for us to let go of?

The penalty is clear here. *"You are cursed with a curse, for you have robbed Me, even this whole nation."* *Malachi 3:9*

> *"Bring all the tithes into the storehouse, That there may be food in My house, And try Me now in this," Says the Lord of hosts, "**If I will not open for you the windows of heaven And pour out for you such blessing That there will not be room enough to receive it.**" Malachi 3:10*

Does that say what I think it says? Does it say if I give, I'll also get. Some would answer, *"No, it doesn't say that because everyone knows that you can't do to get."*

That's ridiculous; religion has imprinted on the minds of many to never expect more; However, God was telling us that the law of increase is tied up in the law of sowing to reap.

Could many have missed this secret key and overlooked what Genesis 8:22 was trying to reveal?

> *"As long as the earth is here, seed time and harvest time will not cease." Genesis 8:22*

Are we blind because of mans traditions? Are we blind because someone told us this is not how it is? It is time to open our eyes to Truth.

The church needs money. For the church to receive the rains of finances we are going to have to open our hands and sow money seeds to receive a money harvest from the Lord.

Some may ask, *"Where should I bring my tithe and offerings?"* We are to bring them to the storehouse. What's the storehouse? Your local church; that's what I believe the storehouse is. The place where you are attending that gives you spiritual food and protection.

Wait there's more! LOOK...

*"And **I will rebuke the devourer for your sakes**, So that he will not destroy the fruit of your ground, Nor shall the vine fail to bear fruit for you in the field," Says the Lord of hosts;   And all nations will **call you blessed**, for you will be a delightful land," Says the Lord of hosts." Malachi 3:6-12 NKJV*

Wow, this is incredible! We give and then we can expect God to find a way to get it back to us. Not only is God going to cause it to rain blessings on me, He's going to rebuke the devourer for me. God is going to take notice when the enemy is advancing on me unnoticed, and God will stand up and rebuke him for me! What a stress free promise. My territory will be safe. **My house... my children... my life... all protected by my willingness to release my tithe and offerings**.

Not only am I protected, everything I do is going to produce and increase for my promotion. I would be a fool not to tithe and give my offerings with this information.

All this has to do with the latter day rain. The former and the latter day rains coming down together. Prepare for your deluge!

CHAPTER THIRTEEN

THE LAW OF RELEASE

DR. JERRY A. GRILLO, JR.

THE LAW OF RELEASE...

*R*ain is all about the law of release. First, the atmosphere warms the earth through the sun and draws the water from the earth to release it back somewhere else on the earth. Think for a moment... The earth in one place is releasing water through evaporation just to release it in another place where it needs it most. The earth is set up to take care of itself. How does it accomplish this? It accomplishes this through the process of sowing to reap. The whole power is the law of release.

> *"So shall My word be that goes forth from My mouth; It shall not return to Me void, But it shall accomplish what I please, And it shall prosper in the thing for which I sent it." Isaiah 55:11 NKJV*

Everything on the earth was set up for the law of release. God spoke this in the beginning... The end shall be revealed from the beginning.

> *"Then God said, "Let the earth bring forth grass, the herb that yields seed, and the fruit tree that yields fruit according to its kind, whose seed is in itself, on the earth"; and it was so. And the earth brought forth grass, the herb that yields seed according to its kind, and the tree that yields fruit,* **whose seed is in itself according to its kind.** *And God saw that it was good. So the evening and the morning were the third day." Genesis 1:11-13 NKJV*

Do you see it? The last part of verse twelve says whose

seed is in itself according to its kind... this is how the earth kept producing what it needed to be more than what it was. The very grass you stand on today is product of the grass that was created in the beginning. It took a portion of itself and released it back to the earth to reproduce; over and over and over until you have the grass, the trees, the bushes and all seed bearing plants around you today. The miracle was attached to the LAW OF RELEASE:

Now, these plants, animals or any other living thing on the earth would have ceased from living if the earth hadn't released its water to the sky so that the atmosphere could release it back on the earth somewhere else.

WANTING MORE IS NOT WRONG! Everything on the earth requires more. The need to eat and drink is the proof that we were created to need and want more. More food... more water... more! Wanting more is not a sin. We've been taught that more is wrong. Most of us, in our religious upbringing, were taught that wanting more was a selfish act. There is a big difference between self care and selfishness.

Self care is what I do to advance myself and my family to a better way of living. It's where you seek to increase yourself through study, working harder and solving problems to be promoted. Self care is a trait that I believe God placed in all of us. It is the need to fight the spirit of mediocrity and to advance to a higher level of living, a higher level of consciousness. This is not an evil act of ambition but a God given drive to be better. Who in there right mind can believe that wanting to be better and to have more is wrong and ungodly? I believe that the person who chooses not to change and doesn't want to be better is a good definition for being called ungodly.

Evil is found in the background of those who don't want to better themselves. I'm not saying that those people are evil, but that evil is found in that way of thinking. The enemy has convinced the mind to accept their lives and not attempt to change it.

Selfishness is when you attempt to increase or better yourself at the expense of someone else. It is destroying those around you in the attempt to build and be better. Selfishness is ignoring others to advance yourself. This is when advancement is wrong, but to advance, increase, want to have more, do more, and be more within itself is not selfishness. This is our God given command to increase... to subdue... to have and take dominion.

> *"Judge not, and you shall not be judged. Condemn not, and you shall not be condemned. Forgive, and you will be forgiven.* **Give***, and it will be given to you: good measure, pressed down, shaken together, and running over will be put into your bosom. For with the same measure that you use, it will be measured back to you."* Luke 6:37-38 NKJV

> *"Do not be deceived, God is not mocked; for whatever a man sows, that he will also reap."* Galatians 6:7 NKJV

Notice these two verses together. Let's understand why rain from Heaven is the best rain. When God rains on us we will reign on the earth. This will require the law of release to be operating in us.

The phrase "GIVE, and it will be given back to you..." We must understand that after you have released your giving, God receives it and then moves his hand of increase on it.

1. **Good measure**
2. **Pressed down**
3. **Shaken together**
4. **Running over**
5. **Men will give back to you**

What is God using to work the law of release and return? Whatever measure you used, the same measure was used to return it back to you. I like to say if you used a teaspoon to release it, God uses a teaspoon to return it. Even with that, you are receiving more than you released. If you decide to work your faith and use a wheelbarrow, God will use a wheelbarrow to return it back to you.

Do not be deceived... don't be tricked or lied too... God will not be mocked. Whatever you sow, or release, that is what you will reap. ***Reaping means to collect, to harvest, to gather, to select, get in and obtain.***

Give and it will be given back to you... would men give into your bosom...

WANTING MORE IS NOT WRONG!

Everything on the earth seems to possess the need for more. I have often thought that wanting more was a wrong feeling. My religious imprinting led me to believe for so long that wanting more was not what a humble loving Christian would desire. Wanting more meant I wasn't happy or that I wasn't content. The scripture that would always run through my mind was being content in whatever situation or circumstance you are in (Philippians 4:11).

After much study and much thought, I've come to the realization that most things on the earth require more. More sun, more rain... more time. Wanting more is a part of life. I was created for more. I was created to have and to be better tomorrow than I am today. This word content means that no matter where I am in life I am not unhappy with my life. However, because Jesus is in me, I can do all things... become all things... accomplish all things... I will succeed in the end. To be content doesn't mean we have to be satisfied with where we are or what we are doing... I am not satisfied with my life. I want more! Everything around me needs promotion; my mind, my home, my children, my church and every area of my life.

Life requires increase. We should be increasing in our prayer life... we should be increasing in our home life... we should be increasing in our information life... we should be increasing in our financial life... we should be increasing in our understanding and wisdom daily. More! More should be what we want everyday. More love! More hope! More Faith! **More Presence!**

How did we drift so far from God's plan for our lives? Look around, read the book of Genesis and you will discover that everything was created for us to live in an unlimited supply of blessing.

RELEASE IS ABOUT UNLIMITED SUPPLY

When reading the story of Abraham in Genesis chapter twelve, I realize that it's not just a story about a certain religion. Three of the biggest religions on the earth trace their heritage back to Abraham. The Jews, Christians and Muslims all claim that the whole Abraham thing is about them; however, there is more to this story than a history lesson on genealogy.

Just for thought; it is 1000 years until Moses is born. 2500 years after Abraham that Jesus is born and 3100 years after Abraham, Mohamed is born and we have the Muslim's religion. This is not to say that Abraham isn't about those things, but it's to say that there's more. We need to look deeper at this story than just birthing religious persuasions.

The whole story is about **unlimited wealth, unlimited resource.**

> *"The Lord had said to Abram, "Leave your country, your people and your father's household and go to the land I will show you. "I will make you into a great nation and I will bless you; I will make your name great, and you will be a blessing.I will bless those who bless you, and whoever curses you I will curse; and all peoples on earth will be blessed through you." Genesis 12:1-3 NIV*

First, to experience a life of unlimited resource you have to be willing to do what Abram did. You must be willing to release where you are to walk into your future; leave to cleave, move from what's familiar to enter a life of the unfamiliar. This is what faith means. It's having enough confidence in the voice of God to follow no matter what, believe no matter what and walk away from everything you know. Learn how to follow God's voice.

You have to understand the power of rain to understand the power of release. Rain is the embodiment of what God's abundance looks like. When rain falls, everything uncovered becomes saturated by it. There's no fighting it. You will become completely soaked with water if you are standing anywhere in the open when it is raining. You will not be able to hide that you have

THERE'S NO HIDING WHEN YOU HAVE BEEN DRENCHED BY GOD'S PRESENCE

been drenched by a down pour. The same is true when God begins to open Heaven and allow it to rain His all consuming power and presence over your life. When this happens there will be no hiding that you have been drenched with His presence and with His abundance.

"The goal of the enemy is to weaken your self confidence."

5 KEYS TO A LIFETIME OF UNLIMITED RELEASE

1. ABRAHAM BECOMES A SURRENDERED LIFE.

Life is a trade off... How would you like to trade your life right now for a better life? I have a friend that says all the time, *"The rest of your life can be the best of your life..."* I believe it! I believe that when you surrender your life to God and accept His son Jesus, you can walk in the power of John 10:10.

> *"I am the door. If anyone enters by Me, he will be saved, and will go in and out and find pasture. The thief does not come except to steal, and to kill, and to destroy. I*

*have come that they may have life, and that they may have it **more abundantly**." John 10:9-10 NKJV*

Let's look at Revelation 12:11; a scripture that I believe teach us live a surrendered life.

"And they overcame him by the blood of the Lamb and by the word of their testimony, and they did not love their lives to the death." Revelation 12:11 NKJV

"They defeated him through the blood of the Lamb and the bold word of their witness. They weren't in love with themselves; they were willing to die for Christ." Revelation 12:11 (The Message bible)

I like the Message Bible. It makes very clear how we are to become overcomers. To live a surrendered life you have to give up the fight with God. You can't live a surrendered life and still do what you want at the same time. The trade off has to be made; your life for His (Jesus) life. This has become an unpopular subject in this twenty-first century society. The American church has a problem with the surrendered message. We are too enamored with what we have and what we can gain; people get very nervous when someone speaks about a surrendered life.

To surrender means to give in, to give up, to lay down your arms, to yield and to submit. These words have become curse words today. To live a life of unlimited wealth... unlimited resources you first have to do what Abraham did... Leave to cleave! You have to walk away from your imprinting of your friends, your country, and if need be, your own family to blindly follow the voice of God. Abraham had to follow this voice. Imagine telling those around you that you are leaving what you know to go places you've never been. What faith. **Faith is reaching out into no where, hanging on to nothing, until it turns into something.**

Three steps to a surrendered life

1. The Blood of the Lamb. I am convinced that the only way to victory is through the name of Jesus. They overcame... they defeated the enemy... they walked in victory because the early Christians possessed and used the name of Jesus. There seems to be a watered down version of Christianity today. People do not have a problem using the name of God, but they do have a problem using the name of Jesus. Why? Because the name Jesus is the only name that holds power and substance.

2. The word of their testimony. The Message Bible gives a clearer understanding to this verse, *"**And by the bold word of their witness...**"* The early Christians were not ashamed to speak up and be counted. They were not ashamed of the Gospel of Jesus Christ. They knew in their hearts it was the only power unto salvation. These early Christians possessed what we need today, boldness! They possessed courage to speak. They had the audacity to be counted and the bravery, valor and confidence to defend their faith even unto death.

3. They did not love their life as their own. This is the surrendered life. They gave up their lives to be counted, to be heard.

2. MOVE SWIFTLY FROM THE ANCHORS OF YOUR PAST.

No one can ever enter their future staying connected to and focused on their past. Abraham was commanded to get out from those things that had anchored him to a certain way of thinking. You will never claim or discover your assignment staying in the same place and talking about things you already know.

I have already been in my past. There's nothing back there I want; however, we have yet to enter our future and that's where the greatest blessings are.

The cheapest form of conversation is *"Remember when..."* I was watching a TV show with leaders sitting in a room around the table. All but one of the leaders was older and had lived through a lot of history. These older leaders all kept talking about the past and remembering when. Noticing that the younger, more vibrant leader wasn't saying much, they asked why he wasn't talking. His reply got my attention. *"The cheapest conversation you can have is 'remember when."* He said, *"We've already been through yesterday... I want to know where we are going... what are we about to conquer, what is our next move. Let's talk about our future."* I loved it!

Ninety percent of most people's conversation time has nothing to do with their future but their past or present problems. You can't move away from your present until you have released the past.

3. UNDERSTAND THAT WARFARE WILL ALWAYS SURROUND A LIFE THAT IS FAVORED AND BLESSED.

The first few chapters of the bible tell us that Cain killed his brother, Abel, after God favored his offering. Joseph's brothers rose up and tried to kill him when God favored him. David's brothers hated him, and King Saul tried to kill him when God favored him. A clue you've been touched by God and have been called to do something is the warfare that surrounds you.

Mary was favored to birth the Messiah, yet her first season of favor was struggle and hardship. She had to be willing to risk her reputation and losing her fiancé. Whoever said that the touch of God is always bliss has never really been touched. The first season of His touch, His favor, is usually a season of struggle and warfare. You qualify for the blessing, for favor, when you endure the season of warfare. You may have to be thrown into a pit, sold into slavery, falsely accused and thrown into prison as Joseph was, but never lose sight that you have been favored. You will rise up and take your place in your greatness in the end. Joseph ended up being the second highest person in Egypt. He went from the pit, to the prison, to the palace. The way to the palace is sometimes very hard and very long. Don't give up... don't complain and lose your praise. Just stay focused on the promises of God. You will become the blessing of the Lord in the end.

Stand, Fight, Win! That's all you have to do at this stage. Don't quit. Remember, Mary had to weather the first season, but after she birthed her promise seed kings, magistrates and others laid gold, myrrh, frankincense and silk at her feet. She became very wealthy. Prepare for WAR!

4. STOP ROAMING AND START OWNING.

God gave Adam and Eve ownership, dominion, when they lived in the Garden of Eden. They were to stay in the Garden and subdue it. They had permanent residence in the presence of God... They were looked after, cared for and protected by their ability to walk in obedience. God gave them ownership to all that was His as long as they stayed obedient. God sent them out of His garden when they decided to take matters in their own hands and do what they wanted instead of what they were told. They were no longer land owners; they became land roamers. They went into a nomadic mind set.

Until Abram, the people were nomadic in mind set; meaning they would move in and occupy the land. Not own it, just use it and all its resources. They would pack their stuff up and move on to the next place when the land couldn't produce for them anymore; only to deplete the next place of all its strength and resources.

WEALTH IS NEVER ATTACHED TO NORMAL!

God called Abram out from the people who were nomadic. This is powerful because Abram became the first land owner in the Bible. God tells him to buy a piece of land for four hundred shekels. Abram was the first person who changed his mind set from roaming to owning.

I believe that nomadic thinking has embedded into the mind set of the American church. They move into a church and drain it of all its resources. When that church, pastor and leadership can no longer supply them what they need, they begin to shift blame onto the leadership and pastor, then move on to the next church. Nomadic in their loyalty, they sap the land of all its resources and then move on; taking no ownership in the land or the church.

God stopped this way of thinking in Abram. Abram began to own the land and learned that if he sowed into that land he could reap what the land released. This gave Abram access to unlimited resources. He no longer had to stress his family and move them all over the land just to sustain them. He could stay in one place and reap from that place. The limit to his wealth was hinged on his inability to sow into the land.

HE BEGAN TO PROSPER; HE CONTINUED TO PROSPER, UNTIL HE BECAME VERY PROSPEROUS.

Genesis chapter twenty-six tells us that the same thing happened to Abraham's son.

"There was a famine in the land, besides the first famine that was in the days of Abraham. And Isaac went to Abimelech king of the Philistines, in Gerar. Then the Lord appeared to him and said:" Do not go down to Egypt; live in the land of which I shall tell you. Dwell in this land, and I will be with you and bless you; for to you and your descendants I give all these lands, and I will perform the oath which I swore to Abraham your father. And I will make your descendants multiply as the stars of heaven; I will give to your descendants all these lands; and in your seed all the nations of the earth shall be blessed; because Abraham obeyed My voice and kept My charge, My commandments, My statutes, and My laws. So Isaac dwelt in Gerar." Genesis 26:1-7 NKJV

"Then Isaac sowed in that land, and reaped in the same year a hundredfold; and the Lord blessed him. The man began to prosper, and continued prospering until he became very prosperous." Genesis 26:12-14 NKJV

Notice that there was a famine in the land and everyone was moving to Egypt. God intervened and commanded Isaac not to do what everybody else was doing. First, you need to understand that wealth is never attached to normal. This is crazy. Stay in a place where famine is.

Famine can be necessary! God can use famine to weed out the non-favored... the non-productive; move swiftly away from those who have not been favored. God can use famine to force those out of your life who don't belong. Wrong people can block and hinder the very hand of blessing. I have heard of stories where people wanted to bless someone but wouldn't, simply because of the friendships those people were connected to.

If Isaac wanted what his father got, he had to be willing to do what his father did. Trust God in the midst of abnormal situations. Crises really don't make, us they reveal us!

Isaac stayed in the land. Here's where ownership begins. Isaac sowed in that land. He dug wells in that land. Wells promote governorship (dominion), and sowing seeds promotes loyalty to the land. Those who don't sow into you, your church or your ministry are probably not with you. People come to church usually for three reasons.

1. *Because there's a reason they are there. They usually leave when the reason is over ...*
2. *Because of a season. They usually leave when the season is over.*
3. *Because they are connected and have lifetime loyalty. These people usually don't leave.*

Isaac sowed in the land and in that same year reaped a one hundred fold return. I like this phrase because it doesn't say in twelve months; it says in that same year! This could mean in twelve months, or it could mean that whatever time he sowed, within that same year he reaped. Just a thought here, what if he sowed in October; he would have received in that same year.

WOW! Unlimited resources are connected to the hand of an unlimited God.

I am sick of hearing people talk about the resources of this earth running out. The doomsayers and negative speakers are trying to put fear in us. I don't believe anything God makes will run out of resources; especially the earth.

Here's the kicker. Isaac began to prosper and continued to prosper until he became very prosperous. That's where we are right now. We are somewhere between continuing and until we become...

5. WORK THE LAW OF RELEASE TO THE FULLEST.

Everything is about release. You can't move into a better life until you release the one you have now. You can't enter your future until you release your past. You can't forgive until you release un-forgiveness and bitterness. Those who are angry about their parents need to release them. The person who is trying to commit in their new church but can't because they are still offended over what happened to them at the last church has to work the law of release. If you don't release one season the next season will not come.

The farmer can't become excited about his harvest until he first releases the seed into the soil. The same is true with you and I. We can't get excited about unlimited wealth... unlimited resources... unlimited health until we work the law of release. We must let go of what's in our hand if we dare to see what's in God's hand.

Wouldn't you love to see what God is holding right now over your life? If so, then release the seed! Go ahead and let it go. What you walk away from, God will walk back into your life pressed down, shaken together and running over.

Abraham did it... Isaac did it... Jacob did it... so on and so forth. If they can unlock the unlimited hand of God because of their willingness to release, so can we.

Remember, whatever a person sows that will he also reap. (Luke 6:38). God will not be deceived; whatever we sow we will reap. Don't allow false religious mindsets to change the word of God and cancel out your harvest. Sow your money... and expect to reap a money harvest... sow your time... expect to reap a time harvest... sow kindness... expect to receive a kindness harvest... Sow mercy... expect to reap mercy!

CONCLUSION:

I sure have enjoyed writing this book. It has been a source of blessing to me. I can honestly say that in writing this book, God has taught me how to open Heaven and expect rain.

Position yourself right now for open heavens. Prepare yourself for the abundance of rain! Remember, unless you're in the right position, God will not open the windows of Heaven and provide you with an outpouring. You will have to settle the rest of your life on the mist of God.

What a tragedy to live in the land of portions when we were destined to live in the land of plenty.

The air rises to develop clouds and produce rain. When God is getting ready to open Heaven and shower us with His abundance, there is going to be something in the atmosphere that causes what has been holding us down to rise. When God arises, His enemies will scatter.

Two feet of water can wash large vehicles away. Water is the best example of the Spirit. It doesn't take a lot of God to do great and marvelous things.

I have labored to create an atmosphere of expectancy for a greater love and walk with God with in you as you read this book. It is my wish and desire that you wake up and stop living in the land of portions. Stop limiting yourself to what others say you can have. I want you to get up and start claiming your right as a citizen of the Kingdom.

It's getting ready to rain! Are you ready for it?

Dr. Jerry A. Grillo, Jr.

SCRIPTURES ABOUT RAIN

"Then I will give you rain in due season, and the land shall yield her increase, and the trees of the field shall yield their fruit." Leviticus 26:4

"That I will give you the rain of your land in his due season, the first rain and the latter rain, that thou mayest gather in thy corn, and thy wine, and thine oil." Deuteronomy 11:14

"My doctrine shall drop as the rain, my speech shall distil as the dew, as the small rain upon the tender herb, and as the showers upon the grass." Deuteronomy 32:2

"And it came to pass at the seventh time, that he said, Behold, there ariseth a little cloud out of the sea, like a man's hand. And he said, Go up, say unto Ahab, Prepare thy chariot, and get thee down, that the rain stop thee not." 1 Kings 18:44

"Who giveth rain upon the earth, and sendeth waters upon the fields." Job 5:10

"Thou, O God, didst send a plentiful rain, whereby thou didst confirm thine inheritance, when it was weary." Psalm 68:9

"Then shall he give the rain of thy seed that thou shalt sow the ground withal; and bread of the increase of the earth, and it shall be fat and plenteous: in that day shall thy cattle feed in large pastures."Isaiah 30:23

"For as the rain cometh down, and the snow from heaven, and returneth not thither, but watereth the earth, and maketh it bring forth and bud, that it may give seed to the sower, and bread to the eater" Isaiah 55:10

"Be glad then, ye children of Zion, and rejoice in the LORD your

God: for he hath given you the former rain moderately, and he will cause to come down for you the rain, the former rain, and the latter rain in the first month." Joel 2:23

"Ask ye of the LORD rain in the time of the latter rain; so the LORD shall make bright clouds, and give them showers of rain, to every one grass in the field." Zechariah 10:1

"For the earth which drinketh in the rain that cometh oft upon it, and bringeth forth herbs meet for them by whom it is dressed, receiveth blessing from God" Hebrews 6:7

END NOTES:

Chapter Nine - some of the information was gathered by *"The Pentecostal Pulpit"* South Eastern College, Music, Praise and Worship July 1993

WHAT SOME ARE SAYING ABOUT
DR. GRILLO

Dr. Jerry Grillo lives what he teaches. It has been my privilege to be his personal friend for a number of years. He is a living example of a victorious leader. His church is a victorious church. If you can't succeed under this man of God you can't succeed anywhere. His revelation is life's fresh air in a stagnant world. He is one of the happiest and most exciting leaders I have known through my thirty-eight years of world evangelism. It is my privilege to commend any book he has written.

> Dr. Mike Murdock
> The Wisdom Center, Dallas, TX.

Dr. Jerry Grillo is truly a gift from God to my life. I love his passion, his purity, and his painstaking commitment to purpose. It is very obvious that he loves the God he preaches to us about. Should you ever have the privilege of peeking into his life, you will find, without a doubt, he's one of God's favorite. Bishop Grillo, what a wonderful refreshing! What a wonderful friend!

> Pastor Sheryl Brady
> Sheryl Brady Ministries
> Durham, NC.

Dr. Jerry Grillo has an important message that is simple, direct and critical for our times. He addresses the most basic issue for the emerging generation, but it is also the crucial message for all ages. It is the message that Jesus came to earth to share with us about the favor of God.

> Pastor Rick Joyner
> Founder and Senior Pastor
> Morning Star Ministries

Decision Page

May I Invite You to Make Jesus Christ the Lord of Your Life?

The Bible says, *"That if you will confess with your mouth the Lord Jesus, and will believe in your heart that God raised Him from the dead, you will be saved. For with the heart man believes unto righteousness; and with the mouth confession is made for salvation."* Romans 10:9,10

Pray this prayer with me today:

"Dear Jesus, I believe that You died for me and rose again on the third day. I confess to You that I am a sinner. I need Your love and forgiveness. Come into my life, forgive my sins and give me eternal life. I confess You now as my Lord. Thank You for my salvation! I walk in Your peace and joy from this day forward. Amen!"

☐ **Yes, Dr. Grillo! I made a decision to accept Christ as my personal Savior today, and I would like to be placed on your mailing list.**

Name_____

Address_____

City_____

State _____ Zip _____ Phone_____

Email_____

FOGZONE MINISTRIES
P.O. Box 3707, Hickory N.C. 28603: 1-888-FAVOR-ME
(328-6763)
www.bishopgrillo.com or www.Godstrongtv.com

BECOME A FAVORED PARTNER

Dear Favored Partner,

God has brought us together... When you get involved with God's plans He will get involved with your plans. To accomplish any vision, it take partnership...It takes people like you and me coming together to accomplish the plan of God.

WILL YOU BECOME ONE OF MY FAVORED PARTNERS TO HELP CARRY THE BLESSINGS OF GOD ACROSS THIS NATION?

"When You Work Your Faith Seasons Change." I have asked God to work with your faith to believe for four harvests when sowing your partner seed.

1. **A Harvest of Divine Health**
2. **A Harvest of Divine Financial Increase and Blessings**
3. **A Harvest of Divine Family Restoration**
4. **A Harvest of Divine Protection**

Sit down and write the first check by faith. If God doesn't increase you in the next months, you are not obligated to sow the rest.

Yes Dr. Grillo, I want to be one of your monthly partners... I am coming into agreement with you right now for my THREE MIRACLE HARVESTS.

Thank you,

FAVORED PARTNER
Dr. Jerry A. Grillo, Jr.

RTNERSHIP PLAN:

300 Favored Champion Partner: Yes, Dr. Grillo I want to be one of your vored Champion Partners of $42.00 a month; involving my seed as one of e 300 who helped Gideon conquer the enemy of lack.

70 Favored Elders: Yes, Dr. Grillo I want to be one of your 70 Favored ders of $100.00 a month. I want to be one of those who will help lift your ms so that we can win over the enemy of fear and failure.

MY Best Seed: Seed Amount $_____.____ Remember, no seed is too nall and all seeds multiply. Seeds of nothing will produce harvests of thing. Send your best seed today.

ame_____ ____

Address_____

City _____State_____ Zip_ _____

Phone _____Email _____

Write Your Most Pressing NEED Below!

_____

_____

_____

_____

FAVORED HONOR ROLL

I want to honor those who sowed into this project. Below are those who have sacrificed to place this book into your hands. Please pray for them daily.

The Favor Center Hickory; Hickory N.C.; Bishop Jerry and Maryann Grillo
Pastor Raymond Hollis and The Favor Center Choir

Marsha Vega
Gerald and Patty Grillo
Bob and Connie Johnson
Jeff, Anna and Joshua Grillo
Daniel Alexander
Doug and Renee Bedore
Ron and Kathy McCoy

April Mercer
Heather Cary
Mike and Erica Hill

Rock Wealth Ministries; Dr. Todd Coontz
Abundant Life COG; Long Island, NY; Pastor Greg and Helen Wilks

Tony and Diane Mauro
Kathy Carbone
Pastor Greg and Helen Wilk
Roger and Lia Echauri
Rebecca Carbone
Andrew Isaac Silva
Rema Stewart
Willam and Teresa Paxton and Family

Fania and Charles Arrowy
Kathleen Holbrook
Louis and Karen Medina
Eric and Denise Olsen
Angel and Mira Valladares
Alexis Echauri
Reanie and Dawn Marie Hveen
Elise fikes

Raymond and Yvonne Hollis
Laurina and williams Anderson
Victoria Woods
Rev. Bertha Colman- Hawkins
Debbie Thomas
Ruth and Leonard Green
Dianna Lyles

Lonniyell Silkes
Junalisa Thompson
Chris Burnett
Dorrey Lyles
Charles and Carol Oglesby
Bonne Davis

Mr. and Mrs. Ron Giordano

Hope Apostolic Church; Cleveland, TX; Pastor Jerry and Sue Mathews
Britanie Cameron
Buddy and Shelee Whitmire
Tammy Fregia
Michael Posey
Fregia Construction
Greg and Sharon Dettling
Eddie Logsdon
Fran Collins
Josh Collins
Donna Dowdell
Jesse and Frances Manning
Deana Walterscheid
Colen Walterscheid
Brittany Walterscheid
Deborah Graham
Mary Doyle

David Fregia
Candace Bush
Chris Bush
Summer Sathe
Gerald and Dianne Lum
Jeanette Morgan
Tina Collins
Justin Collins
William Browning
Karen Whitmire
Bill and Lynette Graves
Justin Toth
Chris and Kerri Waller
Kathy Wilson
Ida Johnston

TO INVITE DR. JERRY GRILLO TO SPEAK AT YOUR NEXT
CONFERENCE , CHURCH OR TO SCHEDULE TELEVISION OR RADIO INTERVIEWS

WRITE TO:

FOGZONE MINISTRIES
ATTENTION: APRIL MERCER
P.O. BOX 3707 HICKORY, NC. 28603

OR EMAIL: FZM@CHARTER.NET

FAX INVITATION TO 828-325-4877

OR CALL 1-888 FAVOR ME